Edward Potts

Fresh water sponges; A monograph

Edward Potts

Fresh water sponges; A monograph

ISBN/EAN: 9783337714000

Printed in Europe, USA, Canada, Australia, Japan

Cover: Foto ©ninafisch / pixelio.de

More available books at **www.hansebooks.com**

FRESH WATER SPONGES.

A

MONOGRAPH,

BY

EDWARD POTTS,

INCLUDING "DIAGNOSIS OF EUROPEAN SPONGILLIDÆ."
By Prof. FRANZ VEJDOVSKY, (PRAGUE.)

PHILADELPHIA:
ACADEMY OF NATURAL SCIENCES,
1887.

CONTENTS.

(In this reprint the paging of the Proceedings of the Academy of Natural Sciences of Philadelphia has been retained for convenient reference.)

Preface:—Scope and purpose of the work: acknowledgements.	158
Introduction:—Elementary information as to Sponges;	160
External appearance;	162
Favorite situations; modes of search;	163
Special subjects for study;	164
Propagation for minute examination of living sponges;	165
Collecting and preserving;	167
Determination of species;	168
Variability of species.	170
Characteristic features of some localities mentioned.	
A New Jersey Cedar Swamp.	185
Fairmount Dam, Philadelphia.	213
Brandywine Creek, Pennsylvania.	229
Mt. Everett, Massachusetts.	231
The Colorado of the West, Mexico.	235
Lehigh Gap, Pennsylvania.	238
River Amazon, South America.	254
Chester Creek, Pennsylvania.	264
Lansdowne Run, Philadelphia.	266
Key to the genera of Fresh water Sponges.	181
Key to the species (17) of the genus Spongilla.	183
Key to the species (17) of the genus Meyenia.	210
Key to the species (4) of the genus Heteromeyenia.	237
Key to the species (5) of the genus Tubella.	248
Key to the species (3) of the genus Parmula.	256
Key to the species (4) of the genus Carterius.	261

Total, 50 species in the *Group* Spongillina: 8 species in the *Provisional Group*.

"Diagnosis of the European Spongillidæ." 172–180
    Condensed Synopsis, Carter's arrangement. 180
Class, Spongida: *Order* Holorhaphidota; *Family*, Potamospongida.
Group, Spongillina; *Genera*:–Spongilla, Meyenia, Heteromeyenia, Tubella, Parmula, Carterius.
Provisional Group; *Genera*,–Uruguaya, Potamolepis, Lubomirskia.

Group SPONGILLINA

              (1) Gen. SPONGILLA.   182

(1) Spongilla aspinosa. 184
(2) Spongilla lacustris. 186
    Spongilla " v. paupercula. 189
    Spongilla " v. dawsoni. 190
    Spongilla " v. abortiva. 191
    Spongilla " v. montana. 192
    Spongilla " v. multiforis. 192
    Spongilla " v. lehighensis. 193
        Syn. *S. canalium, ramosa, lieberkühnii, jordanensis.* 172
        Syn. *Euspongilla lacustris, jordanensis.* 172
        Syn. *S. mutica, flexispina, lacustrioides.* 190, 191
(3) Spongilla rhenana, (*Euspongilla rhenana*.) 174
(4) Spongilla alba. 193
(5) Spongilla cerebellata. 194
(6) Spongilla carteri. 194
(7) Spongilla nitens. 195
(8) Spongilla navicella. 195
(9) Spongilla bombayensis. 196
(10) Spongilla botryoides. 197
(11) Spongilla sceptrioides. 197
(12) Spongilla cinerea. 197
(13) Spongilla fragilis. 197
    Spongilla " v. minuta. 202
    Spongilla " v. minutissima. 202
    Spongilla " v. irregularis. 202
        Syn. *S. lordii* (201), *contecta, siberica, glomerata.* 176
        Sgn. *S. ottawaensis, morgiana, calumeti, segregata.* 197
(14) Spongilla igloviformis. 202
(15) Spongilla mackayi. 204
(16) Spongilla böhmii. 205
(17) Spongilla novæ terræ. 206
    Spongilla arachnoidea. 184
    Siphydora echinoides. 184

(II) Gen. MEYENIA. 210

(1) Meyenia erenaceus. 177, 211
  Syn. *Spongilla erenaceus; Trochospongilla erenaceus.* 177
(2) Meyenia leidyi; (*Spongilla leidyi*). 212
(3) Meyenia gregaria; (*Spongilla gregaria*). 217
(4) Meyenia minuta. 218
(5) Meyenia fluviatilis; (*Spongilla fluviatilis*). 178, 219
  Meyenia " v. meyeni; (*Spongilla meyeni*;) 221
  Meyenia " v. acuminata. 222
  Meyenia " v. mexicana. 222
  Meyenia " v. angustibirotulata. 223
  Meyenia " v. gracilis. 224
  Syn. *Spongilla pulvinata; Ephydatia fluviatilis;* 178
  Syn. *Spongilla asperima, stagnalis, astrosperma, polymorpha.* 219
(6) Meyenia mülleri, (*Ephydatia mülleri*). 177, 224
  Syn. *Spongilla mülleri, Meyenia mülleri, Trachyspongilla mülleri.* 177
  Syn. *Spongilla mirabilis; Ephydatia amphizona.* 177
  Syn. *Pleiomeyenia calumeticus, walkeri, spinifera.* 224
(7) Meyenia bohemica; (*Ephydatia bohemica*). 179, 225
(8) Meyenia robusta. 225
(9) Meyenia millsii. 225
(10) Meyenia subdivisa. 226
(11) Meyenia baileyi; (*Spongilla baileyi*). 227
(12) Meyenia capewelli, (*Spongilla capewelli*). 228
(13) Meyenia anonyma. 228
(14) Meyenia ramsayi. 228
(15) Meyenia crateriformis. 228
(16) Meyenia everetti. 230
(17) Meyenia plumosa; (*Spongilla plumosa*). 233
  Meyenia " v. palmeri. 234

(III) Gen. HETEROMEYENIA. 236

(1) Heteromeyenia repens; (*Spongilla repens*). 237
(2) Heteromeyenia argyrosperma; (*Spongilla argyrosperma*). 239
  Heteromeyenia " v. tenuis. 240
(4) Heteromeyenia longistylis. 242
(3) Heteromeyenia ryderi. 242
  Heteromeyenia " v. pictovensis. 244
  Heteromeyenia " v. walshii. 246
  Heteromeyenia " v. baleni. 247

(IV) Gen. TUBELLA. 248

(1) Tubella paulula; (*Spongilla paulula*). 248
(2) Tubella spinata. 249
(3) Tubella reticulata; (*Spongilla reticulata*). 249
(4) Tubella recurvata; (*Spongilla recurvata*). 250

(5)	Tubella pennsylvanica.	251
	" v. minima.	252
	Syn. *T. fanshawei, T. intermedia.*	252
	(V) Gen. PARMULA.	254
(1)	Parmula batesii, (*Spongilla batesii*).	257
(2)	Parmula brownii, (*Spongilla brownii*).	257
	v. tuberculata.	258
(3)	Parmula rusbyi.	259
	(VI) Gen. CARTERIUS.	260
(1)	Carterius stepanowii; (*Dosilia stepanowii*).	179, 262
(2)	Carterius tubisperma, (*Carterella tubisperma*).	263
(3)	Carterius latitenta.	264
(4)	Carterius tenosperma.	265
	Syn. *Spongilla tentasperma, S. tenosperma, Carterella tenosperma.*	265

Provisional Group.

	(VIIa) Gen. URUGUAYA.	268
(1)	Uruguaya corallioides; (*Spongilla corallioides*).	268
	(VIIb) Gen. POTAMOLEPIS.	269
(1)	Potamolepis leubnitziæ.	269
(2)	Potamolepis chartaria.	270
(3)	Potamolepis pechuëlii.	270
	(VIIc) Gen. LUBOMIRSKIA.	270
(1)	Lubomirskia baicalensis.	270
(2)	Lubomirskia bacillifera.	271
(3)	Lubomirskia intermedia.	271
(4)	Lubomirskia papyracea.	271
	Conclusion.	272
	Description of Plates.	273–279
	Plates V to XII inclusive.	

CONTRIBUTIONS TOWARDS A SYNOPSIS OF THE AMERICAN FORMS OF FRESH WATER SPONGES WITH DESCRIPTIONS OF THOSE NAMED BY OTHER AUTHORS AND FROM ALL PARTS OF THE WORLD.

BY EDWARD POTTS.

PREFACE.

Dr. Bowerbank's "Monograph of the Spongillidæ," (Proc. Zool. Soc., London, 1863 p. 440 etc.) and "The History and Classification of the known species of Spongilla," by H. J. Carter Esq. F. R. S. etc. (Annals and Mag. of Nat. Hist., London, 1881, p. 77 etc.) contain the only complete synopses of the fresh water sponges, as known at their respective dates. Both writers have, in their introductory remarks, given full information as to the history and bibliography of this branch of study, which it cannot be necessary now to repeat.

My design in the preparation of the present paper has been, primarily, to describe those genera and species, mostly North American, that have been discovered since the date of Mr. Carter's publication; next, to detail the results of a somewhat extended examination into the character and variations, in North America, of those species that have long been familiarly known in Europe; and thirdly, to make it valuable for reference as a Monograph, by adding brief technical descriptions of all other "good" species.

A further purpose, and one that I hold much at heart, is the desire to revive, among scientists and lovers of nature, an appreciation of the apparently almost forgotten fact of the existence of sponges in our fresh water; to show them that they are easily found and collected; that they are deeply interesting as living subjects of study, microscopic and otherwise; and that, by simple processes, their typical parts may readily be prepared for classification and the permanent preservation of their various singular forms. With this end in view the situations and conditions in which the American species were found, have been briefly described, suggesting the hopefulness of an exploration of similar localities in other neighborhoods.

During the last six or seven years the leisure time of a very busy life has been largely occupied in the collection and examination of sponge material. In this labor of love I have been greatly aided by the contributions and correspondence of friends, till then unknown, in widely separated districts, for whose thoughtful kindness I now desire to express my indebtedness. It were idle to attempt to name them all; but to Professors Allen, Cope, Hunt, Leidy and Heilprin of Philadelphia, to Dawson, Hyatt, Bumpus and Osborn in other localities, I am particularly indebted. As active workers in the same field and during nearly the same period, I am glad to acknowledge my constant obligation to my friends Mr. Henry Mills, of Buffalo, N. Y. and Mr. B. W. Thomas of Chicago, Ill., whose names will frequently be found throughout the following pages. More recently my valued friend and correspondent Mr. A. H. MacKay, of Pictou, Nova Scotia, has been untiring in his efforts, very successful in his local and New Foundland collections and most generous in the contribution of his valuable material. I owe to my friend Prof. John A. Ryder of the University of Pennsylvania, what has been of more value than any material, the most unfailing courtesy and the best of advice, assistance and encouragement to persevere in my work. From abroad I have been honored with the correspondence and publications of Dr. W. Dybowski of Niankow, Russia, Prof. Marshall of Leipsig, Vejdovsky and Petr of Prague, Bohemia. Prof. Vejdovsky has laid me under especial obligations by his repeated gifts of Bohemian and other European sponges, besides his "Diagnosis of the European Spongillidae" now published as a very valuable contribution to this paper. I thank Dr. C. W. de Lannoy, late of Chester, Pennsylvania, for the original drawings for plates V and VI the excellence of which will be conceded by all acquainted with the subjects.

Two names remain of friends, without whose influence and assistance this Monograph would probably never have been written. The first has passed the alloted term of "three score years and ten," and now, with failing strength, but unfailing love of his work, is hastening to garner the last ripe sheaves of a life of honorable scientific labor. I count it a great privilege to have become acquainted, near the beginning of my work, with H. J. Carter, Esq. of Devonshire, England, than whom no obscure scientist could hope for a more constant friend or more courteous correspondent. To the fine artistic skill and unwearying patience of the other, Miss S. G. Foulke of Philadelphia, my readers, with myself, owe a large part of the value of this work, in the admirable drawings from which plates VII to XII have been reproduced.

These reproductions are the work of the Photo-Engraving Co. (N. Y.) and while it is regretted that from the very nature of the process no photo-engraved plate could repeat, with their relative delicacy, the finer lines of Miss Foulke's beautiful drawings, in other respects they are very well done.

INTRODUCTION.

A few words of elementary information may be desirable to aid those who for the first time undertake the study of sponges.

In constitution and general appearence the fresh water sponges resemble many of those of a marine habitat, excepting in one particular. This crucial point is the presence, during certain resting seasons, in most of the former, and the absence from *all* the latter, of those "seed-like bodies" that have been known and described by various authors under the names of ovaria, gemmules, statoblasts, statospheres, sphærulæ, etc. In the past I have generally avoided the use of the familiar word statoblast, as it did not seem clearly proven that the function of these "seed like bodies" of the sponges was identical with that of the statoblasts of the polyzoa etc; and have used the terms statospheres, or sphærulæ, as suggesting merely their general appearance. Latterly, however, I have concurred with several European writers in the use of the old term, gemmules; the principal objection to which, is that with some persons the name may seem like a return to the exploded vegetable theory of sponges. It is hardly necessary to say that this idea is not intended.

In shape these gemmules are nearly spherical; they are about $\frac{1}{50}$ of an inch in diameter, or as large as very small mustard seeds. They are found sometimes in continuous layers, as at the base of encrusting sponges; sometimes they rest singly in the interspaces among the skeleton spicules; again, they occur in groups of a dozen or less, sparsely scattered through the sponge mass, or in smaller, denser groups, closely enveloped in a compact cellular parenchyma. Their principal coat, presumably of chitin, encloses a compact mass of protoplasmic globules, each of which is charged with numbers of discoidal particles, whose function, though all important, it is not my intention to discuss in the present paper. A circular orifice, rarely more than one, through this chitinous coat, sometimes, though inaptly called the hilum, should be known as the foramen or foraminal aperture. Through it, at the time of germination, the above mentioned protoplasmic bodies make their exit, crawling by an amœboid movement, and spreading out on every side. In a few hours the infant colony may be seen producing aqueous currents, developing and arranging skeleton spicules, and in every way living the life of a young sponge. The foraminal aperture is rarely plain; more frequently it is infundibular, (Pl. V, fig. i, a,), having a slightly raised and expanded margin; while in still other species it is prolonged into cylindrical or funnel shaped tubules (Pl. VI, fig. iii, iv, and v.)

In most species, possibly in all under normal conditions, the chitinous coat is surrounded by a "crust" (Pl. VI, figs. i, ii, etc.), composed of air cells, often so minute as to be with difficulty "resolvable," even with a high power of the microscope; in other species so large as to be readily discerned by the use of a low one. In the first instance it has been called a "granular," in the other, a "cellular" "crust." In this are imbedded (Pl. V and VI,), the spicules which, as will be hereafter seen, are relied upon to determine the generic classification of these sponges.

To recur for a moment to the resemblance stated to exist between the fresh water and *some* of the marine sponges,—we can see no obvious reason why *all* the marine forms should not have their representatives among those belonging to fresh water; but it is a fact that all of the latter, as yet discovered, are *silicious;*—that is, the skeleton or framework, (corresponding to the elastic fibre of which commercial sponges are composed) upon which the slime-like sponge flesh, known as "sarcode," is supported, and through whose interstices the currents meander, is composed of silicious spicules, slightly bound together by an almost invisible quantity of firmer sarcode or perhaps of colloidal silica.

To form the main lines of this skeleton structure the spicules, averaging about $\frac{1}{100}$th. of an inch in length, are fasciculated in bands made up of several spicules, lying side by side, and somewhat overlapping at their extremities; the crossing lines being formed of more slender fascicles, or even of single spicules. In the different species these "skeleton" spicules vary in size, in the shape of their terminations, and in their more or less spinous character (see Plates VII to XII, a,a.); but while these differences serve, in some degree, as specific guides, they are not sufficiently constant or positive to form a basis for generic arrangement.

Besides the skeleton spicules, a second class, known as "dermal" or flesh spicules (Pl. VII to XII, c, d, e, etc.) is found only in some species and in greater or less numbers, either lying upon the outer "dermal" film or lining the canals in the deeper portions of the sponge. They are almost always much smaller than those of the skeleton and are never fasciculated or bound together in any way. A third class of spicules is composed of those before mentioned as imbedded in the "crust" of the gemmules, and form what may be regarded as their armor or defensive coating. These gemmule-spicules represent two principal and several subordinate types, which have been selected by Mr. Carter to define the different genera into which he has divided the single genus *Spongilla* of the earlier authors. His method of classification will be given later.

The sponge in its entirety as a growing organism can generally be easily recognized by the collector, after he has escaped from the thraldom of the idea that any fixed growth, of a more or less vivid green color, must be a *plant* of some kind. Of course the mosses and confervae will be rejected after examination, upon the evidence given by the leaves of the one and the smooth slender threads of the other. If doubts remain as to any specimen, the presence in it of efferent or discharging apertures, like those of the commercial sponge, if it is really a sponge, may serve to dispel them, and still more convincing proof will be given by the use of a pocket lens, in detecting the points of multitudinous spicules thickly studding the surface. When, in addition to these guiding features, the spherical gemmules just described are found within or under it, there should be no further hesitation.

The green color spoken of, is common and characteristic; yet it is not universal, but closely dependent upon the quantity or quality of the light received. When a sponge has germinated away from the light and has grown upon the lower side of a plank or stone, it will be found nearly white, gray or cream colored. As it enlarges and creeps around the edge and up into the full sun light it assumes a delicate shade of green, deepening as the exposure increases, till it attains a bright vegetable hue. Even in the sunlight, however, some species are never green. (See description of *Meyenia leidyi*.)

These organisms have occasionally been discovered growing in water unfit for domestic uses; but as a rule they prefer pure water, and in my experience the finest specimens have always been found where they were subjected to the most rapid currents. The lower side of large, loose stones at the "riffs" or shallow places in streams: the rocks amid the foaming water at the foot of a mill-dam fall; the timbers of a sluice-way, the casing of a turbine waterwheel, or the walls of a "tail race" beneath an old mill;—in all these places they have been found in great abundance and of a very lusty growth. Of all discouraging situations it is almost hopeless to look for them in shallow water having a mud bottom. Mud is their great enemy, as gravity aids their natural currents to fill the cavities with earthy matters that soon suffocate them, because the latter are too feeble to throw them off. Of course in any body of water liable to be charged with sedimentary material, the principle of natural selection favors those growing on the lower side of their bases of support, which protect them from the intrusion of the heavier particles.

For that reason perpendicular and water logged or floating timbers, submerged stumps of trees, and branches drooping into the water from trees or bushes along the banks, are favorite locations. They do not disdain more temporary support, such as weeds and water-grasses. I have received from a friend, specimens growing upon water plants that wild ducks had torn from the bottom, and that were found floating upon the surface of Lake Michigan. Through the clear water of our northern lakes, we may often see them lying in slender lines upon the leaves of submerged weeds, or in beautiful cushion-like masses upon the stones or gravel.

In my explorations I have had much satisfaction in the use of a long pole, to which was attached a small net, with one part of its edge shaped into a scraper, like a garden hoe. This enabled me to examine the surface of timbers at a depth of eight or ten feet and to tear off and bring up sponges from that depth; beyond which all is to me an "aqua incognita." Biologists labor at some disadvantage in studying the fauna of our fresh water, as compared with the facilities offered them in collecting ocean subjects. The nets and dredges of many exploring expeditions have, at least, *begun* to acquaint us with the inhabitants of the "deep sea;" but who knows anything about the fauna or the flora of our deep fresh-water lakes, or even of our larger streams? The largest specimens of this group ever reported, were dredged from the bottom of Lake Baikal in Central Asia, (*Lubomirskia*). I know of no similar attempts to collect them elsewhere. It is to be hoped that means may be found ere long to make such explorations, which must result in an increase of knowledge in many lines. Meantime no opportunity offered by the accidental or designed drainage of artificial reservoirs should be neglected. I have spent hours of great pleasure and profit while groping around the distributing reservoirs upon Fairmount Hill, Philadelphia, at times when the water was drawn off for cleaning or repairs.

One further point as to methods of collecting and I shall finish this section of my subject. Unless our sponges are large, it is difficult to detach them without mutilation, from the rough surfaces of stones. It is therefore preferable to gather, when possible, those growing upon wood, which may be scraped or chipped without injury to them. It is essential to secure the very lowest portions, as it is there the gemmules often abide.

The proper season for collecting fresh water sponges, in waters of the temperate zone, depends upon the purpose of the collector. If it is his desire to gather cabinet specimens merely, for the identification of old or the determination of novel species, it is hardly worth while to begin before July. As with the flowering of plants, the maturity of different species of sponges is attained at various dates, between mid-summer and late in November. The essential point is, that the gemmules and their armature shall be fully perfected; and when that condition is attained in any specimen, there is no reason for further delay.

I would, however, recommend to intending students a far higher object for their ambition;—that is, the study of the physiology and life history of sponges as members of a sub-kingdom whose position has been greatly questioned and whose character, derivation and subsequent evolution are very important and perplexing topics. I would have such workers search for and examine them at all seasons of the year, (even in midwinter, when I have never failed in suitable situations to find some in a growing condition), keeping memoranda as to each species separately; noting the date of their germination or earliest appearance, the locality, elevation, temperature; rapidity of growth at different seasons; time and manner of formation of gemmules; stability or decadence during the winter; modes of distribution and progression, whether always down stream or by other more adventitious methods; what becomes of the gemmules upon reaching salt-water, and the thousand and one problems that go to make up the life history of any animal form, and that, in this instance, have been very little studied. I am particularly anxious that some competent person should undertake their study in the briny, brackish and the fresh water lakes, pertaining to what is known as the "Great Basin of the West," with a special view to ascertain the conditions under which they form "protected gemmules" in such localities. By this means, light may possibly be thrown upon the problem of their possible derivation from the marine sponges.

Great pleasure and profit may be attained in the same direction, by germinating the statoblasts or gemmules under artificial conditions, and studying the development of the young sponges by the aid of as high powers of the microscope as the ingenuity of each student may bring to bear upon the subject. I take the liberty to copy from the Ann. and Mag. Nat. Hist. 1882, p. 365, Mr. Carter's directions for germinating statoblasts, which will be found valuable. "To obtain the young spongillæ it is only necessary to get a portion of an old living specimen bearing statoblasts, and, having taken out a few (six to twelve) of the latter, to roll them gently between the folds of a towel to free them from all extra material as much as possible, place them in a watch glass so as not to touch each other, with a little water, in a saucer or small dish filled with small shot to keep the saucer upright and, covering them with a glass shade, transfer the whole to a window bench opposite to the light. In a few days the young *Spongilla* may be observed (from its white color) issuing from the statoblast and gluing the latter as well as itself to the watch glass, when it will be ready for transfer to the field of the microscope for examination, care being taken that it is never uncovered by the water, which may be replenished as often as necessary; but of course the object-glass (when ¼ inch with high ocular is used for viewing the minute structure) must admit of being dipped into the water without suffusion of the lens."

My own first experience in the propagation of fresh water sponges may prove instructive in various ways. Late in the autumn of the year 1879, in a pond within the "Centennial Grounds," Philadelphia, I found for the first time a living sponge. It was a vigorous, branching specimen of *Spongilla lacustris*, charged with gemmules in all parts of its structure. A fragment firmly attached to a stone was taken home and placed in a gallon "specie-jar" with water, in the hope, begotten of inexperience, that it would continue to grow, exhibit its inflowing and exhalent currents, etc. On the contrary, and as I now know, almost necessarily, it died, and in a few days the water became insupportably foul. It was changed and another trial made, which resulted as before. This time the jar was thoroughly cleansed; the stone with the attached sponge was taken out and held long under a flowing hydrant before it was replaced in the jar, which was now left in an outer shed and, very naturally, forgotten. Weeks passed and winter came on, and one severe night the water in my jar was frozen solid and the vessel fractured. I supposed that the low temperature to which it had been subjected would prove fatal to the germs, but, as the specimen was a fine one, it seemed well to save it, even in its skeletonized condition. So, when its icy envelope had been melted off, the sponge was again thoroughly washed until all the sarcode was removed, when, in a fresh jar, it again became a parlor specimen.

I do not clearly remember when signs of germination were first observed. It was probably in January, as during that month I find that artificial conditions very frequently bring about the hatching of such animal germs as those of the polyzoa etc. I detected first a filmy, grayish-white growth that seemed associated with the detached gemmules which lay in the groove around the bottom of the jar. A gray, featureless growth at first,—then spicules were seen, in slightly fasciculated lines, attached to the glass and reaching upward, then spreading out fan-like and branching. These were of course, covered with sarcode, nearly transparent at first, and through the filmy surface pores and osteoles could be detected with a pocket lens. The latter were surmounted by the so-called "chimneys" or cone-shaped extensions of the dermal film ; and through the apertures at their summits effete particles could almost constantly be seen, puffed out, as if thrown from a volcano and then blown off by the wind.

These products of single gemmules did not, as time passed on, greatly increase in size ; possibly, because of deficient nutriment in the unchanged water of the jar: but, crawling upward along the glass to an average height of an inch or less, left the naked spicules in place behind them as so many ladders or "stepping stones of their dead selves" by which they had reached to "higher things." Near the summit, one or more new gemmules would sometimes be formed, after which the mother mass entirely disappeared.

So much for the amount of growth from single gemmules. Where, however, they were thickly sown, or germinated *in situ* upon the stone, so that the contents of several could mingle and flow together, the resultant sponge was very much larger. The mass, if it may be so called, covered, at its best, nearly one third the surface of the jar; while those gemmules remaining upon the stone and amongst the spicules of the old sponge, continued to germinate, to form abundant sarcode and spicules, and, at least in one place, to throw out a long unsupported branch or finger-like process, that ultimately reached a length of two or three inches.

Of course it was impossible to bring the higher powers of a compound microscope to bear upon a sponge growing under such circumstances; a strong Coddington lens was the best that could be applied to this work ; but a very fair share of success was obtained by the device of scattering small squares of mica among the growing gemmules, which, when covered by the young sponge, could be removed to the stage of my instrument, covered with water in a compressorium and examined comparatively at leisure. It was a perpetual cause of astonishment to me, to see so large a production of silicious spicules from a single gallon of water, in which the chemist would probably have failed to find any such constituent. It is worthy of consideration however, whether such silica as composed the older spicules may not, at least when under the influence of the growth force of the younger sponges, be to some extent soluble.

Further observations regarding the late maturity and the winter growth of some sponges will be found recorded in the general remarks concerning *Spongilla aspinosa, S. lacustris* etc.

As to processes of gathering—I have already mentioned the advantages obtained by the use of the "scraper net" in relatively deep water and in connection with perpendicular timbers etc. At depths of two feet or less, great facility of action is gained by wearing high rubber boots and wading after our specimens, to pick from the bottom stones, sticks or pieces of waterlogged timber, under which they may be concealed. Where the water is deeper, of course a boat must be used, to approach the floating, submerged or dependent sponge-bearing substances. A large, strong knife or a paperhanger's scraper will be found convenient for hand work at short range. A case containing trays an inch or so in depth is suitable for carrying the smaller specimens; the larger will of course require vessels of greater size. On reaching home or headquarters it is well to select some specimens of characteristic shapes and containing gemmules, for storage in dilute alcohol, making use of wide mouthed bottles to avoid crushing them. The rest may be spread upon boards in sheltered situations, in the shade (for the sun bleaches them rapidly) and left to dry; turning them every few hours to prevent decomposition. If time is limited or the specimens are large, artificial heat may be necessary; but, whatever process is used, the drying must be *thorough*, or mould will soon cover the sponges with a mycelium which may be beautiful enough in itself, but is far from agreeable or sightly as a feature of the sponge. Whether they are to be dried or preserved in alcohol, they should be dealt with promptly and on no account left to lie long in the water after being gathered. Preserve from dust in covered boxes.

For the determination of species, a few general directions may suffice, and even these will be soon modified to suit the tastes or the ingenuity of the worker.—It is assumed that the investigator has already noted the general appearance of the sponge in hand; its color, size, compactness; whether simply encrusting, or cushion like; sending out finger-like processes etc. These indications may help an experienced collector to a guess; but there are very few species that even such a one could name, with any confidence, before he had made and examined microscopic preparations of the same.

A stand, supporting a dozen or more test tubes, say three fourths of an inch in diameter by an inch and a quarter in depth; a dropping bottle containing nitric acid, and the usual materials and apparatus for mounting in balsam, are all the appliances needed. As the processes to be described are certain to disturb the normal relations of the several classes of spicules to each other, it is well before the dried specimen has been much handled, to separate some clean portions of the outer or dermal film, lay them upon a slide and mount in balsam without further preparation. An examination of this may determine the presence and decide the character of the dermal spicules, if there are any pertaining to the species in hand. This precaution is necessary in view of the displacement of parts just mentioned, and also on account of the indiscriminating habit of the sponge-currents during life, which almost necessarily charge the tissues with various foreign particles, including vagrant spicules of its own and neighboring species. In practice, the rightful presence of dermal spicules in any species is often so doubtful, that it can only be settled by an examination of young sponges, grown under observation, from isolated statoblasts, whose identity has been satisfactorily determined.

Next, separate from the sponge some minute fragments, containing skeleton spicules, the dermal and interstitial tissues and a dozen or more gemmules. Place several of the last named with a few adherent skeleton spicules upon the centre of a fresh slide,—bring to the boiling point in one of the test tubes, five or six drops of nitric acid and by the aid of a dropping tube apply a single drop of the hot acid to the gemmules upon the slide. While the acid is partially destroying their cellular or granular crust, pour the remaining fragments into the acid left in the test tube and boil violently, until all the tissues are destroyed and the spicules left as a sediment upon the bottom of the tube. Fill up the tube with water and stand it aside to settle; which may take an hour or more. The few minutes that have elapsed will probably have been as much as the gemmules upon the slide will bear; they must not be left so long as to destroy the chitinous coat, nor is it well, though a common practice, to *boil them upon the slide* for this often smears and disfigures it with frothy matter. Remove most of the acid by trickling drop after drop of water over the slide while held in a slightly inclined position. Wipe off all the water that can be reached and apply repeated drops of strong alcohol to take up the remainder. When this is so far accomplished that the gemmules will absorb benzole freely and receive their covering of benzole or chloroform balsam without *clouding*, apply the balsam and a cover glass. This process of removing moisture by the use of alcohol, rather than by drying over a lamp, is preferred, although it requires more care and time, because the gemmules are less likely to be distorted in shape and the cells of the crust to become filled with air, if they are kept always under fluid. Yet if the mounted gemmules, when examined, appear black, showing an accidental intrusion of air, much of this can be removed by carefully heating the slide over a lamp.

If this mount has been successful, the gemmules are now so transparent that their surrounding spicules can be readily seen and the genus determined, by the aid of the "Key" hereafter given; but a better view of the detached spicules is necessary, and may be obtained by mounting some of the contents of the test-tube. If the lately suspended spicules have now settled, carefully pour off all the water except one or two drops; though if there has been much acid used it may be better to wash them a second time. Shake up and place a sufficient quantity upon one or more slides, being careful not to leave the contained spicules in too dense a mass. I have found it best to allow the water to evaporate from these slowly; as, if hurried over a lamp, each spicule is often margined with minute globules that it is impossible afterward to remove. However, when the slide is apparently quite dry, it may be safely exposed a moment to the heat, to make sure of it, and then covered with balsam and glass as usual.

The investigator has now before him all the elements necessary for solving his *specific* problem, according to the formulæ which follow:—the normal sponge, the dermal film, the transparent gemmule, and a display of the detached spicules. Neither would alone answer, but the series will settle all points, excepting in the case of the genus *Carterius*. When this is suspected, the gemmules should first be examined *dry*; and, in preparations for mounting, great care should be taken to avoid the destruction of the tendrils, (cirri) (Pl. VI, figs. iii, iv, v. and vi), by the prolonged use of strong acid. Expert microscopists will improve their gemmule mounts by dividing some of them with a thin knife, endeavoring to make the section through the foraminal aperture; this, in the case of species having long birotulates, such as *Meyenia crateriformis*, (Pl. V, fig. vi,), is of the utmost importance.

"Seniors" in microscopy will please pardon the minutiæ of the processes just given, as they were necessary to make them available for the "freshmen." All are reminded that the above directions as to collection and examination refer to mature sponges only. It is seldom safe, or even possible, to *name* one, in which no gemmules can be found. If a course of study is undertaken, involving the histology and physiology of fresh-water sponges, many peculiarities will of course be observed that have not been alluded to here. One of them concerns the development of the spicules and, if not understood, will pretty certainly mislead the beginner into the supposition that he is examing a novel species. Both the skeleton and dermal spicules of *young sponges* are frequently marked with bulbous enlargements at the middle and often half way between the middle and each end of the spicule. These seem to indicate an immature condition, as they disappear when the spicules are fully formed.

A few words may be needed to justify the specific groupings I have adopted. I am well aware that objections may be made to so large a use of what some will call a "trinomial nomenclature." Without expressing an opinion as to the policy of the practice as regards other branches of the animal kingdom, in the case of the sponges I think it clearly unavoidable; for the reason, that the inert parts that have just been described as typical, share with the vital amœboid cells, their well known characteristic of unlimited variability. Were all the names that have been dropped or marked as varieties to be recognized as full species, on the ground that the specimens so designated do not exactly resemble any others, the literature would be encumbered with a mass of names representing forms that no description could distinguish, and no one of which would probably entirely correspond with the next specimen collected by its author from the same stream. This variability in forms that were considered typical when the first of a species was collected and named, is a fact in science that will not fail to impress any who may gather from many waters and through a wide extent of country.

Among some very incomplete memoranda of my collections and receipts, I find it recorded that I have examined *Spongilla fragilis* from at least 32 localities in 18 North American States; *S. lacustris*, from 26 localities in 16 states; *Meyenia fluviatilis* from 25 localities in 14 states; *Tubella pennsylvanica* from 18 localities in 11 states etc. Had a perfect list been kept, the figures might be largely increased. And this is the lesson most obviously taught:—hardly any two specimens are exactly alike in their so-called typical features; but all may be *grouped*, as in the case of those brought together under any of the above designations, and common definitions or descriptions will, without undue elasticity, cover them all. The varieties I have retained are such as were originally considered good species, and have generally some slight peculiarity to recommend them; but to the student I would say, "Get your genus right and your species right, and then it will matter little whether you associate it with any variety."

The following "Diagnosis" was prepared at my request by Prof. Franz Vejdovsky, of the University in Prague, Bohemia, to give information as to the number of reliable species of fresh-water sponges known by students at the present time to inhabit European waters, with their proper synonomy etc., and is far more reliable than I could hope to make it from the scattered literature of the subject. Professor Vejdovsky has greatly aided my work by thus furnishing, in manuscript, a German translation from his Bohemian text; for the English version of which I am further indebted to my friend Prof. Benjamin Sharp of the Academy of Natural Sciences of Philadelphia. As the classification adopted differs from that of Mr. Carter, which, for many reasons, I prefer to follow, it has seemed to me best to present the paper *as a whole* in this place, instead of collating the species and distributing them amongst my descriptions. Due reference will, however, be made to all in their proper order according to Carter's system.

DIAGNOSIS OF THE EUROPEAN SPONGILLIDÆ.

Translated from the Bohemian of Prof. Fr. Vejdovsky, in Prague.

Fam. SPONGILLIDÆ

(A)—*Sub-Fam.* SPONGILLINÆ, *Carter.*

"Gemmulæ, sometimes single and sometimes collected into groups; generally surrounded by an air-chamber-layer, in which the gemmulæ spicules are embedded.

(I) Gen. **SPONGILLA**, Auct.

With long, smooth skeleton spicules and short, either straight or curved, smooth or rough parenchyma spicules. Gemmulæ either entirely smooth or with an external air-chamber-layer, in which the gemmulæ spicules are either tangential or radial, or entirely irregularly embedded.

(a) Sub-gen. **EUSPONGILLA**, Vejdovsky.

Gemmulæ always single. (Besides the European species, most of the exotic species to which Carter gives the generic name of *Spongilla* belong here.)

(1) **Euspongilla lacustris**, Auct.

Syn.— *Spongilla lacustris,* (?) Linn.
1788   "   *canalium,* (?) Gmelin.
1816   "   *ramosa,* (?) Lamarck.
1842   "   *lacustris,* (?) Johnston.
1853   "   "   Lieberkühn.
1866   "   "   Bowerbank.
1870   "   *lieberkühnii,* Noll.
1877   "   *lacustris,* Vejdovsky.
1877   "   *jordanensis,*   "
1881   "   *lacustris,* Carter.
1882   "   "   Dybowski.
1883   "   (*Euspongilla*) *lacustris,* Vejdovsky.
1883   "   "   "   *jordanensis,*   "
1883   "   *lacustris,* Retzer.
    Var. *spon. lacustris ramosa,* Retzer.
      "   "   *lieberkühnii*   "
1884   *Euspongilla lacustris,* Wierzejski.

Diagnosis:—Colony (Stoccke) branched or cushion-like, grass-green, yellowish or brownish. Osculæ and pores indistinct but everywhere numerous. Skeleton spicules, straight or slightly curved, sharp pointed, smooth and enclosed in bundles in a horny sheath. The parenchyma spicules are present in variable numbers, generally moderately curved and set thick with fine spines; at times, however,

when few in number they are smooth. Gemmulæ almost entirely
naked, without the external air-chamber-layers, and with very few
spicules. In other cases they are covered to a greater or less depth
with a layer of minute cells filled with air. At times this layer is
surrounded with a distinct horny membrane, although it is often
wanting. In the air-chamber-layer are imbedded either radially,
tangentially or very irregularly, the gemmulæ spicules, which resemble the parenchyma spicules in external form and variability as
to numbers. Ordinarily they are curved and thickly spined ; rarely
entirely smooth.

Remarks.—*Euspongilla lacustris* is found in nearly all Europe,
as an inhabitant of both running and still water. As the above
Diagnosis shows, these fresh water sponges are liable to great variations, especially in external form, and in the quantity, as well as
the form, of the parenchyma and gemmulæ-spicules. Based on
these variations, *Euspongilla lacustris* would be divided into many
species and varieties. Without doubt we have here a very variable
fundamental (grand) type, out of which new species are beginning
to form. Future careful researches, principally by experiment,
will show where lies the cause of the above mentioned variability in
the form and quantity of the parenchyma and gemmulæ spicules.

Let us first examine those forms that have been looked upon as
indicating distinct species.

We may take as typical, that form in which there are but few parenchyma spicules in the tissues, and in which the gemmulæ are per-
fectly smooth and but sparingly supplied with covering spicules (Belegnadeln). This form of *Euspongilla lacustris* has been regarded by
Lieberkühn, and partly by Bowerbank, as the real *Spongilla lacustris*; and I have also considered it such, in my paper "Die Süss-
wasser Schwämme Böhmens" and so it is also represented by Retzer.
In my "Monograph" I have, however, at the same time, pointed out that
in one and the same colony (Stoecke), other forms are found with
rough parenchyma spicules and with covering spicules (Belegnadeln)
and seem to indicate a transitional stage towards those that have
been looked upon as distinct species.

The nearest of these is *Spongilla leiberkühnii* described by Noll
(Zoologischer Garten) in 1870, and also by Retzer, who, under the
same name, described it as follows:—"Forms encrustations on wood
and stones, from which rise, frequently free, cylindrical processes as
long as one's finger. Skeleton spicules smooth, gradually pointed,

bound into fascicles, which are either long threads, or are placed as a network in the tissues. Hooked spicules cover the gemmulæ and are widely dispersed through the tissues. They live in ponds and quiet flowing water and appear to be the most widely distributed species of Germany."

Although from this description of Retzer's it is evident that *Spongilla lieberkühnii* only slightly differs from his *S. lacustris*, I thought it necessary to examine for myself the nature of the form in question. From a small fragment of *S. lieberkühnii* for which I must thank Prof. Eimer, I clearly recognize its identity with *S. lacustris*. In the form of the gemmulæ and the scarcity of the covering spicules I find no difference between them; sections of the gemmulæ prove that the air-chamber-layer is more or less developed and its surface may be with or without a horny membrane; which is also the case with *Euspongilla lacustris* in various localities in Bohemia.

The immense, even predominating quantity of the strong, rough parenchyma spicules, and an equally large number and variety of the external form of the gemmulæ spicules—these are, on the other hand, the striking characteristics which strongly suggested the recognition of a similar form from the Jordan Pond, near Tabor, in Bohemia, as a distinct species, (*Euspongilla jordanensis*). But the quantity of sponge material that has been at my disposal for some years, convinced me otherwise. In some specimens from the Elb, near Königgrätz and from a pond near Poiakek (?) I found the gemmulæ and covering spicules to correspond with each other, and with the characteristic type of *S. lacustris*; while in single branches, they were identical with the same features in *E. jordanensis*, from the Jordan Pond; and at the same time a corresponding quantity of rough parenchyma spicules was found in its tissues. We must therefore unite *E. jordanensis* with *E. lacustris*.

E. lacustris, var. *macrotheca*, very nearly resembles the following species.—

(2) **Euspongilla rhenana.** Retzer.

Syn.— 1883 *Spongilla rhenana*, Retzer.

This interesting species was first described by Retzer in the following terms:—"It differs from the other species by the *smooth* gemmulæ spicules."

"It encrusts pieces of wood, bushes and the like, sending out a few small processes; and also in many places forms thick masses. The skeleton spicules are straight or slightly curved, abruptly or more gradually pointed. Their thread-like fascicles form a compact network. The gemmule spicules are *smooth*, symmetrically bent near each end, and form a thick layer around the gemmules; but are sparingly distributed through the tissues. The gemmule have a tolerably thick outer wall and are found everywhere in the sponge."

"*Habitat*:—Altrheim (?) near Eggenstein, (in the vicinity of "Karlsruhe). According to Prof. Nüsslin, whom I thank for the specimens, the sponge when living is green, and at all times can be found on fascine bushes (*Faschinen gestraeuch*.")

Through the kindness of Prof. Eimer in Tübingen, I was enabled to examine a fragment of *Euspongilla rhenana*, and can offer some additions to the description of Retzer.

The gemmulæ have the form and size of those of *E. lacustris*, but the polar aperture (*mikrodiode*) is surrounded by a broad, plate-like funnel. Upon the chitinous membrane is a very thin air-chamber-layer consisting of 2–3 cells overlying one another. This layer was rarely deeper than 5–6 cells in a column. The latter support the greater number of spicules. They generally lie tangentially upon the surface of the gemmule and very few are embedded radially in the air-chamber-layer. In shape these spicules are very variable, and generally three principal forms can be determined. The most plentiful are those which resemble the common skeleton spicules; a very few, those mentioned by Retzer, are bent double and such are also scattered singly through the parenchyma; finally, there are found upon the surface of the gemmulæ, spicules that are slightly bent and compressed in the centre.

The auxiliary apertures (neben-mikrodioden), numbering 3–6, upon the surface of the gemmulæ, are worthy of notice. About every tenth gemmule has, near the principal aperture, some lateral funnels; which fact makes this form resemble the species described by Carter from British Columbia, under the name of *Spongilla multiporis*.

(b) Sub-gen. SPONGILLA, Wierzejski.

From 2–30 gemmulæ as a rule, grouped in a common covering, or placed pavement-like along side of one another. Mostly there is a deep air-chamber-layer, through which smooth and rough spicules are scattered.

(3) **Spongilla fragilis,** Leidy.

Syn.—
1851	*Spongilla fragilis*,	Leidy.
1863	"	*lordii*,	Bowerbank.
1870	"	*contecta*,	Noll.
1878-84	"	*siberica*,	Dybowski.
1883	"	*contecta*,	Retzer.
1884	"	*fragilis*,	Vejdovsky.
1885	"	*lordii*,	Wierzejski.
1885	"	*fragilis*,	"
1885	"	"	Petr.
1886	"	*glomerata*,	Noll.

Colony not branched; pale or brown in color, with large oscula which, as a rule, are grouped in large cavities of the surface. Pores numerous and small. Skeleton spicules, nearly straight or but slightly bent; sharp-pointed, smooth, not rarely thickened in the middle. Gemmule spicules numerous, straight or curved, with many minute spines. Gemmule small, spherical, with a high, generally horn-shaped, polar tube, which is filled with air and projects from the air-chamber-layer; the latter consists of large, radial rows of cells. The groups of gemmule, according to the species (?) and the place of development, present two principal forms;—the basal groups are shallow; and here the gemmule are placed pavement-like, close together; those formed in the parenchyma consist of 2 or 3—30 and even more gemmule, forming spherical or hemispherical masses.

This species, *S. fragilis*, first described by Leidy, in America, was later described in Siberia by Dr. Ben. Dybowski, and finally by Noll, as *S. contecta* (and *S. glomerata*). Recently it has been observed in Russia, (in Donec (Donetz?) near Charkow), in Galicia, Bohemia and England and has been described repeatedly by Dybowski, Retzer, Carter, Vejdovsky, Wierzejeski and Petr.

(B) **Sub-Family, MEYENINÆ,** Carter.

Gemmule generally single, surrounded by an air-chamber-layer in which amphidises are embedded in one or more series, one above another. They are either star-shaped or have entire margins.

(II) Gen. **TROCHOSPONGILLA,** Vejdovsky.

With smooth, (*T. leidyi*), or rough, (*T. erenaceus*), skeleton spicules; amphidises smooth with entire margins, embedded at the base of an air-chamber-layer. Only one species has been found in Europe.

(4) Trochospongilla erenaceus, Ehrenberg.

Syn:—
    1846 *Spongilla erenaceus,* Ehrenberg.
    1856   "   "   Lieberkühn.
    1877   "   "   Vejdovsky.
    1881 *Meyenia*   "   Carter.
    1883 *Trochospongilla erenaceus,* Vejdovsky.
    1883 *Spongilla*   "   Retzer.
    1885 *Trochospongilla*   "   Wierzejski.

Trochospongilla is of considerable dimensions, covering foreign bodies in cushion-like incrustations; of a whitish or straw yellowish color; skeleton spicules sharply pointed at both ends; surface, except at the extremities, covered with powerful spines. Parenchyma spicules, correspondingly (?) small, smooth, and very often swollen in the middle. Gemmulæ covered with spool-like amphidiscs whose rotules have entire margins. They lie at the base of a deep air-chamber-layer which consists of radially placed hollow columns, that are divided into a number of chambers by cross-partitions.

Trochospongilla erenaceus has been observed in many places in Europe. In Germany by Ehrenburg; in Bohemia by Vejdovsky; in Galicia by Wierzejski, and in Russia by W. Dybowski.

(III) Gen. EPHYDATIA Gray. Lamarck.

Skeleton spicules either entirely smooth or entirely rough; though sometimes both forms are present together. In the air-chamber-layers, around the gemmulæ, are embedded amphidiscs with star shaped rotules, in one, two or three layers placed one over the other. In the first instance they may be of equal length, but frequently their lengths are unequal.

(5) Ephydatia mülleri, Leiberkühn.

Syn:—
    1816 *Spongilla pulvinata,* Lamarck.
    1856   "   *mülleri,* Lieberkühn.
    1877   "   "   Vejdovsky.
    1878 *Trachyspongilla mülleri,* Dybowski.
    1882 *Meyenia* No. 2.
    1882 *Ephydatia* No. 2.
    1883   "   *mülleri,* Vejdovsky.
          From A. Form B. var. *astrodiscus,* Vejdovsky.
    1883 *Ephydatia amphizona,* part.
    1883 *Spongilla mirabilis,* Retzer.
    1885 *Meyenia mülleri,* Wierzejski.
    1886 *Ephydatia*   "   Petr.

Colony cushion-like, rarely branched, bright green, yellow, yellowish-brown or white, with large osculæ, which lead to a system of small canals. The skeleton spicules are either entirely smooth or entirely rough or both forms are found together in the same colony. Their degree of roughness is very different, as the spines are sometimes quite indistinct, at others very conspicuous. The spicules are either straight or slightly curved; sharp pointed and fasciculated within a horny sheath. The gemmules are surrounded with shallow apertures, slightly flattened from above downward through air-chamber-layers of greater or less depth. Amphidises numerous; ordinarily in a single layer, but sometimes in two layers (*E. amphizona*) and occasionally in three layers (*S. mirabilis*), set one over the others. In the last case the external layer forms an imperfect or broken series of amphidises. The axes of the amphidises are short, relatively to their thickness; the rays either smooth or notched on their edges.

Ephydatia mülleri is known in Europe, in Germany, Bohemia, Russia, Galicia, and England.

(6) **Ephydatia fluviatilis**, auct.

Syn:—

1788	*Spongilla fluviatilis*,	(?)	Linn.
1788	"	*canalium* (?)	"
1816	"	*pulvinata* (?)	Lamarck.
1842	"	*fluviatilis* (?)	Johnston.
1856	"	"	Lieberkühn.
1863	"	"	Bowerbank.
1867	*Ephydatia*	"	Gray.
1877	*Spongilla*	"	Vejdovsky.
1881	*Meyenia*	"	Carter.
1882	*Ephydatia*	"	Dybowski.
1883	"	"	Vejdovsky.
1883	*Spongilla*	"	Retzer.
1884	*Ephydatia*	"	Wierzejski.
1886	"	"	Petr.

Amorphous, cushion-like colonies of an emerald, or bright Isabella-yellow color. Skeleton spicules smooth throughout, slightly curved and sharp-pointed. Parenchyma spicules (?) also smooth, small and very slightly bent. Gemmulæ small, yellow with a thick horn-membrane; the external air-chamber-layer surrounded by a thin chitinous covering. In this layer toothed amphidises are embedded, having either smooth or spinous shafts that are constricted in the middle and twice as long as the diameters of the rotulæ.

In Europe *E. fluviatilis* is found in France, England, Germany, Bohemia, Galicia and Russia.

(7) **Ephydatia bohemica,** F. Petr.

Syn.— 1886 *Ephydatia bohemica* F. Petr.

Colony very small, green, and is found living (parasitic or symbiotic) in the colonies of *Euspongilla lacustris*. Skeleton spicules straight or slightly curved; at times covered with fine spines. Parenchyma spicules numerous, straight or somewhat bent, covered with spinous processes as in *Carterius stepanowii*. Gemmulae with large apertures (mikrodioden) whose pole is expanded into a broad, irregular funnel. In the air-chamber-layer are embedded amphidiscs of equal lengths; some of which, however, project above the surface of the gemmulae. Their shafts are slender and longer than the diameter of the nearly regular, star-shaped, terminal discs. The rays of those discs are finely notched. Rarely does the mikrodiode funnel run into a lengthened tube.

Ephydatia bohemica is, as yet, found only in one place in Europe, viz: in Kvasetic near Deutschbrod in Bohemia.

This species is very characteristic, as it has a certain relationship to, if it is not a transitional form of the following genus *Carterius*; in the fact that the amphidiscs are indistinctly of two lengths; and the tendency shown though rare, for the mikrodiode to lengthen into a polar tube, which is so characteristic in *Carterius*.

(IV) Gen. CARTERIUS, Potts.

Syn.— *Dosilia*, Dybowski, Gray.

Skeleton spicules smooth; those of the parenchyma spinous. Gemmulae with a deep, straight air tube which terminates in an irregular, lobulated disc.

In the air-chamber-layer are embedded amphidiscs of two lengths; one set being as long as the thickness of the air-chamber-layers; the others, just as numerous (?), as the former, project beyond the surface of the gemmulae.

(8) **Carterius stepanowii,** Petr, (Dybowski.)

Syn.—
1863 *Spongilla baileyi*, (?)Bowerbank.
1881 *Meyenia* " (?) Carter.
1884 *Dosilia stepanowii*, Dybowski.
1881 *Carterius* " Petr.

Colony slender, branching, fine to fibrillar, (?) surrounding the stems of water plants. It is of a bluish-green color; dimensions insignificant. Skeleton spicules smooth, straight or curved, sharp-pointed. Parenchyma spicules numerous, bent or straight and thickly set with spines, which are largest at the middle of the spicules. Gemmulæ marked by a polar air tube which is straight or slightly bent, and terminated by a wavy, lobulated disc. The air-chamber-layer is formed of numerous small cells. Amphidiscs of two lengths, of which one third or even a half may project beyond the surface of the air-chamber-layer. The amphidiscs are thickly set with spines.

Carterius stepanowii was first discovered in a lake near Charkow in Russia, and was in 1885 found in Bohemia by F. Petr, in a pond near Deutschbrod."

The above paper of Prof. Vejdovsky has been copied in full, as a very valuable statement of the present status of the specific study of fresh water sponges in Europe, more particularly upon the continent.

SYNOPSIS.

Of the plan of Classification proposed by H. J. Carter, F. R. S. etc., (Ann. and Mag., Feb. 1881) already referred to, he says:—" I found it necessary to make the fresh water sponges the fifth family of my sixth order of the *Spongida* generally, under the name of "*Potamospongida*," with a single group, at present named "*Spongillina*." Hence so far they will stand thus:—

Class SPONGIDA.
Order VI, HOLORHAPHIDOTA.

Char. Possessing a skeleton whose fibre is entirely composed of proper spicules, bound together by a minimum of sarcode. Form of spicule variable.

Family 5, POTAMOSPONGIDA.
Freshwater Sponges.
Group 19, *SPONGILLINA*.

Char. Bearing seed like reproductive organs called statoblasts."

To the five genera named by him, two have been added, to define some recently discovered American types, so that the list now stands.

Genera:— 1. *Spongilla*; 2. *Meyenia*; 3. *Heteromeyenia*; 4. *Tubella*; 5. *Parmula*; 6. *Carterius*; 7, *Provisional*, (the possible material for a new group including *Uruguaya*, *Lubomirskia*, *Potamolepis* etc.)

As has been intimated, these genera have been founded upon the peculiarities of the gemmule-spicules, except in one instance, which is determined by other appendages of the gemmulæ. Assuming that the illustrations will sufficiently show the meaning of the special terms used, the student is referred, without further preface to the following "Key," by comparison with which he will without hesitation be able to decide the *generic* status of his specimen.

Fuller definitions will be given as each genus comes under notice.

KEY TO THE GENERA OF FRESH-WATER SPONGES. Carter's System.

1. Gemmulæ surrounded by acerate (Pl. VII c.c.c) or cylindrical (Pl. VII b.b.b) spicules alone. (Plate V, figs. i, ii, iii.)   SPONGILLA.

2. " surrounded by birotulate (Pl. IX. fig. iii. b.b.b etc.) spicules of a *single* class or type,[1] resting by one (the proximal) rotule upon the chitinous coat; diameters of the rotules equal or nearly so. (Pl. V, fig. iv, v and vi.)   MEYENIA.

3. " surrounded by birotulate spicules of *two* classes or types, both resting by one rotule upon the chitinous coat; the less numerous class longer than the other. (Pl. VI, fig. i,) (Pl. XI. b.c. etc.)   HETEROMEYENIA.

4. " surrounded by inæquibirotulate spicules (Pl. XII fig. i, ii, and iii. b.c.d. etc.) of which the proximal rotule is much larger than the distal one. (Pl. VI. fig. ii.)   TUBELLA.

5. " whose "crust" is charged with spicules from which the distal rotule has been entirely eliminated, leaving the proximal rotule surmounted only by a short, pointed portion of the shaft. (See Ann. and Mag. 1881, Pl. 5, figs. 1 and 2.)   PARMULA.

6. " whose foraminal tubules are prolonged, their terminations broadly funnel-shaped or divided into cirrous appendages of varying numbers and lengths. (Pl. VI. figs. iii, iv, v and vi.)   CARTERIUS.

---

[1] Specimens are occasionally found with birotulates of a *single* type arranged in two or three concentric series. For this form Mr. H. Mills proposed (Proc. Am. Soc. of Microscopists, 1884) the new genus *Pleiomeyenia;* while Prof. Vejdovsky has *merged* two species named on account of the same peculiarity into the common species *E. mülleri*. See "Diagnosis."

7. Sponges in which no gemmule have yet been discovered and whose classification may therefore be considered doubtful. *Uruguaya*, Carter, (Ann. and Mag. etc. 1881. p. 100 and Pl. VI. fig. 17.); *Lubomirskia*, Pallas. *Potamolepis*, Marshall, (Zeit. für Naturwissenschaften XVI. N. F. IX Bd and Taf. XXIV.)

(Particular attention is invited to the illustrations, from plates prepared by the Photo-Engraving Co. (N. Y.). Plates Nos. V and VI are from original drawings by Dr. C. W. de Lannoy, and represent either the whole or portions of gemmules, with their associated spicules, to explain the typical characteristics of the different genera. They are variously magnified as suited his several subjects. Plates VII–XII incl. are also from original drawings, magnificently executed by Miss. S. G. Foulke. They include altogether thirty-six separate groups, representing every class of spicules, in an equal number of species or varieties, all equally magnified and drawn to scale. They may therefore be relied upon as depicting the spicules as the student himself will see them; neither diagrammatic nor idealized. The power used was 400 diameters, which has been reduced upon the plates to one half, say 200 diameters.)

(The measurements accompanying the descriptions of nearly all the North American species are averages resulting from micrometric measurement of from 15 to 30 individual spicules, and may be conviently reduced to millimeters by moving the decimal point two places to the right and dividing by four. The variability in different specimens is so great that I cannot regard any measurements as of exact specific value.)

(I) Gen. SPONGILLA, Carter.

Part of old genus *Spongilla*, Auct. (Plate V, figs. i, ii and iii.)

Gen. Char. Skeleton spicules acerate, generally smooth, curved, fusiform, pointed; mostly accompanied by flesh spicules. Gemmulæ globular; crust variable in thickness or absent altogether; accompanied by or charged with minute acerates, (Pl. V, b.b.b. also Pl. VII b.b.) smooth or spined, imbedded in or lying upon it or on the chitinous coat. Modified from Carter.

When the old genus *Spongilla* of authors was sub-divided by Mr. Carter in 1881, this term was very appropriately restricted to that type which includes the species most widely diffused and most frequently noticed throughout the world.

The following brief summaries of specific points may serve as a guide to the intending student, enabling him at a glance to select the species which his specimen most nearly resembles, without having to read many pages of inapposite matter. (It must be remarked in explanation of the omission of some names, that the verbal descriptions of some of the older species, as copied from their authors, fail to give diferential points that can be made use of in this connection. In the treatment of my own discoveries or those of others that have come to me for examination, I have desired to be thoroughly conservative, grouping those together that have an undoubted relation to one another and not creating either species or varieties unless they appear necessary to aid in study of the subject. I hesitate however to drop species, the type specimens of which I have never seen; although it is probable some of them might become synonyms to advantage.)

KEY TO THE SPECIES OF THE GENUS SPONGILLA.

(a) *Sponge branching.*

1. Slender, cylindrical, waving branches; dermal spicules minute *smooth* acerates; gemmules few, sponge evergreen. (Pl. VIII (fig. vi.) *S. aspinosa.*
2. Branches generally tapering, rigid; less frequently cylindrical and flaccid; skeleton spicules smooth; dermals pointed, spined acerates; gemmules *after maturity* numerous; with or without granular crust; spicules cylindrical, curved, spined. (Pl. VII, figs. i-vi.) *S. lacustris.*
3. Branches small; crust of gemmules thin, spicules *smooth.* *S. rhenana*

(b) *Sub-branched.*

4. Spines of dermal spicules longest at the centre; gemmule spicule round-ended, covered with recurved spines. *S. alba.*
5. Short compressed branches; gemmule spicules at various angles. *S. cerebellata.*

(c) *Sponge without branches.*

6. Gemmulæ with thick crust of polyhedral cells arranged perpendicularly; spicules of gemmulæ *smooth.* *S. carteri.*
7. Crust as in the last species; a layer of minute spined acerates intervened between it and the chitinous body, besides that which is exterior to it. *S. nitens.*

8. Spicules of gemmulae very short, trapezoidal. Gemmule adherent, elliptical; aperture terminal.
S. navicella.

9. Capsule around the gemmule, and chitinous body both spiculiferous. *S. bombayensis.*

10. Shafts of gemmule spicules smooth; heads composed of numerous short blunt or subacute spines. *S. botryoides.*

11. Gemmule spicules spined, particularly near the head.
S. sceptrioides.

12. Color cinereous. *S. cinerea.*

13. Gemmules in layers or groups; apertures *upward* or *outward;* surrounded by a cellular parenchyma, charged with subcylindrical, spined spicules. (Pl. V fig. ii.) (Pl. VIII figs. i to iv.)
S. fragilis.

14. Gemmules in hemispherical groups; apertures *inward;* surrounded by a parenchyma of *unequal* cells, charged with coarsely spined spicules, nearly as long as the less strongly spiniferous skeleton spicules. (Pl. V, fig. iii.) (Pl. VIII, fig. v.)
S. igloviformis.

15. Resembling the above, but with spines more broadly conical, etc. *S. mackayi.*

16. Parasitic on *S. niteus,* with minute, curved dermal *birotulate.*
S. böhmii.

17. Gemmules very large, chitinous coat thin; crust absent or inconspicuous; gemmule spicules smooth, or irregularly furnished with very long spines, frequently located near the extremities. Numerous dermal *birotulates.* *S. novæ terræ.*

(a) *Sponge not branched.*

(1) **Spongilla aspinosa,** Potts. (Pl. VIII, fig. vi.) Proc. Acad. Nat. Sci. Phila. Nov. 1880, p. 357 etc.

Sponge green, encrusting, thin; upon a relatively thick basal membrane; thence sending out numerous radiating, long, slender, cylindrical branches, occasionally subdividing: texture very loose; surface rather smooth, pores conspicuous.

Gemmules very few in scattered bunches of ten to twenty or more, small, spherical, with a granular crust, surrounded by an irregular mass of spicules, resembling those of the skeleton.

"*Spongilla arachnoidea,*" named by H. James-Clark (Am. Journ. Sci. 1871 p. 426), and "*Siphydora echinoides*" by the same author ("Mind in Nature" p. 41, 1865) are not accompanied by such descriptions as will enable me to classify them intelligently.

Skeleton spicules smooth, straight or slightly curved, rather abruptly pointed; an occasional one acuate or malformed.

Outer dermal film charged with minute, straight or curved, smooth, slender, gradually pointed acerates.

Approximate measurements.—Diameter of gemmules 0·02 inches. Skeleton spicules 0·0113 by 0·00033 inches. Length of dermal spicules 0·00144 inches.

Habitat. Upon logs and timbers several feet below the surface of clear standing water, or upon sphagnum, grass, weeds etc. near the surface.

Locality. Collected at Doughty's Pond, Absecum, New Jersey; Brown's Mills, N. J.; Deep Creek near Portsmouth, Virginia etc.

Remarks.—This sponge was first collected by Mr. E. P. Cheyney, a very acute observer, during the summer of 1879 or 1880 in one of the Cedar swamps, near the New Jersey coast. In October 1881, the writer himself collected it, and since that date it has been the subject of frequent and careful observations. Doubt was at first felt as to whether the apparent branches were really self-supporting; but this was long since set at rest and the species is now seen to stand securely *near S. lacustris*, but not *of* it. Some interest may be felt in the following description of its favorite and characteristic locality.

The S. E. portion of the State of New Jersey is, for the most part, a broad sandy plain, not greatly elevated above tide level. It was formerly covered by a dense growth, chiefly of "scrub" pines, and was known as the "Pine Barrens." The few depressions through this district form water courses, along which the drainage of the surrounding neighborhood creeps sullenly, through jungles of cedar mingled with maple, magnolia, and other deciduous growths. Just before Absecum Creek, which has thus wandered for miles through densely wooded cedar and maple swamps, finally loses its identity in the "Thoroughfare," that winds for many a mile among the still flatter marsh lands that line the coast, a low mill-dam checks its course, and forces it to spread its clear, dark waters over acres of refreshing pools, dotted with reed-fringed islets. Here, in clumps, grow the curious leaves and umbrella-like flowers of the American Pitcher Plant; on the margin of the pond are many orchids, those most aristocratic of flowers; in the hollows the *Droseras* or Sundews are doing their best to entrap a few of our insect enemies. The trees, that, years before, had darkened the glen with their shade, killed by the too abundant water, now stand gaunt and desolate above it, "bearded with moss" that hangs and flutters from their otherwise naked branches.

At many places in this beautiful pond the fallen timbers, waterlogged at depths of three to six feet, are lined for yards with this sponge; sometimes only as a smooth, green, enveloping sheet, but at other places reaching out long, radiating branches for six inches or more, swayed delightfully by the clear current. Not only in the "perfect days" of June or through the heats of mid-summer, is the sponge thus verdant and thrifty; but when December has robbed the lake of most of its vegetable forms,—even after February has for weeks covered it with a thick sheet of ice, the sponge has been seen still green and apparently in as healthy growth as ever.

Concurrently with this evergreen habit, we notice the unusual scarcity of gemmules at all times of the year, and feel warranted in inferring that, gifted as it is with this ability to with-stand a low temperature in its growing state, it does not *need* to form "protected gemmules" to conserve its life during hybernation.

In the microscopical study of *S. aspinosa*, the distinctive feature is, undoubtedly, the presence upon the dermal film and amongst the generally smooth, slender, skeleton spicules, of great numbers of minute *smooth* acerates. These are not altogether uniform in size, however; and enough of an intermediate character are occasionally seen, to suggest the possibility that they may be merely initial and immature conditions of the skeleton spicules. The continued perennial growth of the sponge, makes this supposition the more probable; as there is no season in which, as in the case of most other sponges, it may be said to have reached maturity or completeness. In some preparations of it, aborted forms of skeleton spicules are found in considerable numbers and spherical or discoidal masses of silica, without spinous prolongations, or with but a single spine, are not infrequently met with.

(2) **Spongilla lacustris**, Linn. (Pl. V, fig. 1; Pl. VII.)

"Branched; branches long, round and sharp-pointed. Color dark brown, structure fibrous. Skeleton spicule curved, fusiform, gradually sharp pointed, smooth; sometimes more or less spiniferous. Flesh spicule thin, curved, fusiform, gradually sharp-pointed, spined throughout. Statoblast when fully developed globular; crust composed of granular cell-structure, charged with more or less curved, minute, stout, fusiform, sharp pointed acerates, covered with stout recurved spines, arranged tangentially, or centrifugally, like the lines of a so-called "engine-turned" watch case." Carter, (Ann. etc. 1881.)

    Syn. European:—See Vejdovsky "Diagnosis" under *Euspongilla lacustris*. p. 172, etc.
    Syn. American:—
      1863 *Spongilla paupercula*, Bowerbank.
      1863   "   *dawsoni*   "
      1875   "   *flexispina*, Dawson.
      1879   "   *lacustrioides*, Potts.
      1880   "   *abortiva*,   "
      1880   "   *mutica*,   "
      1880   "   *montana*,   "
      1881   "   *multiforis*, Carter.
      1884   "   *lehighensis*, Potts.

As this is the most widely known of all the fresh water sponges, and deserves a full and careful treatment, besides the analysis of it given by Prof. Vejdovsky, under his name *Euspongilla lacustris*, I have also copied Mr. Carter's description above, and now append the result of my own observations, founded upon collections in all parts of this country.

As found in infinite numbers of situations and variety of forms in North America, this sponge is green, when growing, as it does by preference, in the light: from a sessile base freely and repeatedly branching; branches cylindrical or more or less tapering; bristling with the points of radiating spicules; ends of the branches pointed or rounded. Texture loose; the branching processes made up of thick longitudinal lines of fasciculated spicules, united by single spicules or more slender fascicles, in a radiating manner. Pores numerous, large.

Gemmules sub-spherical, often scarce until late in the year, (November) when they are formed quite plentifully in the interspicular spaces, not only in the sessile portion, but throughout the branches of the sponge. Granular crust of the gemmules very variable in thickness; in some forms altogether wanting. Foraminal aperture infundibular.

Skeleton spicules curved, fusiform, gradually sharp pointed, almost uniformly smooth.

Dermal or flesh spicules variable in number, but generally very numerous; curved, fusiform, gradually tapering to sharp points; densely and entirely spined.

Gemmule spicules generally cylindrical, much and variably curved; somewhat sparsely spined; spines more numerous near the extremities, where they are long, acute, and frequently recurved. Upon the gemmules they vary from a horizontal to a nearly erect position, according to the thickness of the crust, and for the same reason are sometimes wanting and at others very numerous.

Hab. On stones and timbers everywhere; preferring running water.

Measurements. Diameter of gemmules 0.02 inches. Average length of skeleton spicules about 0.0108 inches.

Remarks.—*Spongilla lacustris* is certainly not introduced in this connection on account of any claims I desire to make as to authorship or discovery; but rather in the way of recantation or confession that in times past I have so frequently mistaken this name-child of the great Linnæus, clucking to it as one of my own little brood. Indeed it is to save others from a similar experience that I am particular to make this identification.

This species was one of the earliest known; though for years the distinction between it and *Spongilla* (now *Meyenia,*) *fluviatilis* was far from clear. It has been found in nearly all parts of the world where any sponges have been discovered. While many of the fresh water sponges appear to shun the light *S. lacustris* comes out boldly and flourishes in the full sunshine. For this reason and because of its resultant brilliant green color and its conspicuous branching habit, this sponge is better known than any other, and is more frequently gathered by the non-expert collector. I have received it from nearly all my correspondents in the United States and from almost every locality in which any have been collected.

In every place it prefers rapidly running water, where its growth is strong and vigorous. Perhaps my finest specimens were gathered at a place in Chester Creek, Pennsylvania, where the stream was narrowed to a width of ten or twelve feet, rushing between large masses of rock, many of which were coated with the sessile sponge and beautifully fringed with tapering finger-like processes, one half inch or more in diameter by several inches in length. In standing pools, on the contrary, it grows in slender cylindrical branches; as in the subsiding reservoirs on Fairmount Hill, Philadelphia, where it appears in slender, flaccid, yellow-green branches, with hardly sufficient vitality to support themselves above the mud, slowly gathering around them.'

While *S. lacustris* is extremely variable, as to some particulars, upon this continent, (as Prof. Vejdovsky describes it to be also in Europe), in *essentials* the synonyms I have named resemble one another and the European type. These essentials, for comparison, I again describe as follows:—

1st. In general appearance, a green, branching sponge.
2nd. Skeleton made up of smooth, fasciculated spicules.
3rd. Dermal or flesh spicules, *fusiform acerates, entirely spined*, pointed.
4th. Gemmule spicules, whether few or many, generally *cylindrical*, more or less curved, rather sparsely spined, spines often recurved, acute.
5th. Gemmules either apparently wanting or abundant throughout the sponge; with or without granular crust.

As all the sponges above named will bear this description, I cannot see sufficient reason for separating them from the typical form, but many for grouping all together. Some, whose peculiarities are most conspicuous, will be briefly described as varieties.

S. lacustris, var. paupercula, Bowerbank. Proc. Zool. Soc. Lond. 1863 p. 470.

"Sponge coating and branching; surface smooth. Oscula and pores inconspicuous. Dermal menbrane aspiculous (?). Skeleton spicules fusiform-acerate, stout and rather short. Interstitial membranes aspiculous. Ovaries globular, smooth; spicula acerate, small, few in number." Bowerbank.

Loc. Water pipes of Boston, Mass.

S. paupercula, Bk. is, perhaps, that one of this group of synonyms about whose identity with *S. lacustris* there may be most hesitation. Its character is somewhat anomalous, as its locality and associations are peculiar. (See remarks as to *M. fluviatilis, v. acuminata*.) Growing originally in the ponds and reservoirs tributary to the Boston water-supply, it moved forward, and even so early as 1856 Prof. J. W. Bailey wrote to Dr. Bowerbank that "it grows abundantly in the water pipes (aqueducts?) by which the city of Boston is supplied with water from a small lake"; adding a suggestion as to the

---

[1]This is thus far the only instance in which I have found any sponge apparently growing upon a mud bottom; and even here it was doubtless planted upon something firmer, and the length of its branches was probably induced by the effort to lift itself up into greater purity and freedom.

possible diminution of the water way and contamination of the drinking water by its further growth.

I have not had an opportunity to examine the type specimen from which the above description by Dr. Bowerbank was prepared, but from the study of fragments received from Mr. Desmond Fitz-Gerald, Chief Engineer of the Boston Water Department, collected by him from Farm Pond and Cochituate Reservoir, near the head of the water system of that city (in all probability the same that Dr. Bowerbank describes), I am induced to class this as one of the many varieties of *S. lacustris*. In the dry state the sponge is very friable and its dermal surface soon crumbles off, which may in a measure account for the apparent absence of dermal and interstitial spicules from Dr. B's specimens. Mr. H. J. Carter records the finding of acerate, dermal spicules in those received by him from the same locality, and I have found them, though few in number, in the fragments sent to me. We may regard, therefore, the dermal and interstitial surfaces of *S. paupercula* as not *aspiculous* and assert that those found are not entirely smooth; as in nearly all a few spines may be discovered, particularly near the extremities.

* The gemmule spicules are equally scarce and without pronounced character; their *relative* smoothness and greater proportionate length than in most other forms of this species are the noteworthy points. The gemmules are quite numerous, large and entirely devoid of "crust." Their shrunken contents, appearing through the transparent, crustless chitin, give them a peculiar waxen cast. It will be noted, as has before been incidentally mentioned, that in this, as in other cases, a paucity of gemmule spicules attends, as a necessary consequence, the absence of an enveloping crust.

S. lacustris, var. **dawsoni,** Bowerbank. Proc. Zool. Soc. London 1863 pg. 467.

"Sponge sessile, branching; surface smooth. Oscula and pores inconspicuous. Dermal and interstitial membranes abundantly spiculous; spicula fusiform-acerate, entirely spined; spines numerous, short and conical. Skeleton spicula acerate or sub-fusiform-acerate. Ovaria spherical; dermal spicula numerous, disposed in flat fasciculi or groups of spicules parallel to each other (?); groups irregularly dispersed; spicula acerate or sub-cylindrical, entirely spined; spines numerous, obtuse and ill defined. Sarcode aspiculous. Color in the dried state emerald green." Bowerbank.

S. flexispina, Dawson. Syn. Canadian Nat. and Geol. Sept. 1875.
S. lacustrioides, Potts, Syn.

This name was at first suggested under the belief that a distinct specific difference existed between the European and the American forms; an idea that has long since been given up. I now think the resemblance of these forms is quite as close as that of most of those grouped under this name in North America.

S. mutica, Potts, Syn.

This term was applied to an ordinary form of *S. lacustris* during the earlier part of my explorations, before I had learned that it was a very common habit of this species to be without both "crust" and gemmule spicules.

S. lacustris, var. abortiva, Potts.

The name *abortiva* was given to a form of *S. lacustris* first noticed at Fairmount Dam, Philadelphia, in which careful examination during the summer and autumn months of several years, had failed to discover any gemmules. About the 22nd of November 1883, however, upon again collecting the sponge in its original locality, I found, in one instance, the green sarcode leaving the lines of skeleton spicules and collecting in spots, where, a few days later, were found well defined but immature gemmules, entirely smooth and of a vivid green color;—a feature that lasted all winter. Some fragments in this condition were brought into the house and the warmth of the room was found not merely to retard the completion of the gemmules, but in many cases, to reverse the flow of the amoeboid particles, which began to reform and rebuild the skeleton frame-work.

To quote from my note book of that date;—"The appearance of the sponge as now found, was as if the cells of green sarcode had congested or gathered together from their normal position upon the supporting spicules and had just formed immature statoblasts with a very delicate chitinous covering and as yet without either a granular crust or embedded spicules. The skeleton spicules in most cases were entirely bare and the statoblasts bright green." Of another specimen of the same sponge it is remarked.—"This resembled the last mentioned gathering, except that in some places the statoblasts were merely localized by a gradual flowing together of the green sarcode into spots; and the globular shape and chitinous coat of the gemmules had not yet been attained."

The whole of this observation has been of great interest to me first, as indicating the necessity of caution in accepting statements, asserting the entire absence of gemmules from sponges collected by indifferent observers from remote districts, where their life history has never been followed;—next, from the light thrown upon the character of these bodies;—that they are probably neither ova nor ovaria, in any proper sense; but may be *gems* or gemmules, just as, in the vegetable world, we regard the buds of trees, bulbs, tubers etc;—places where the vital particles of the animal or the plant retire for protection during the winter season and for successful distribution in the spring: further, that this act is coincident with the disappearance, at least partially, of the sarcode from those parts of the sponge where the gemmules are found; and that it takes place in different situations and with varying species, at widely different seasons of the year.

S. lacustris, var. **montana,** Potts. (Pl. VII, fig. vi.) Proc. Acad. Nat. Sci. Phila. 1880 p. 357.

This variety was first sent to me by Prof. E. D. Cope, as collected in the well known Lake near the Mountain House on Catskill Mts., N. Y., at an elevation popularly stated to be 2500 feet above tide. Afterward, at my request, Dr. J. G. Hunt kindly sought for and found it at the same locality. As received from the latter collector the sponge was bright green with slender cylindrical branches.

Gemmules quite numerous throughout the sponge; often naked, but also frequently covered by a thick crust and an abundance of spicules, that are placed in a nearly erect position, embedded in the crust.

Skeleton spicules long, very slender, cylindrical, abruptly pointed.

Dermal spicules apparently very scarce, slender, minute acerates; entirely spined. (None are represented in the drawing.)

Gemmule spicules slender, cylindrical; more sparsely spined; spines erect, long, cylindrical; terminations rounded.

Meas. Diameter of gemmules 0.015 inches. Skeleton spicules, 0.0096 by 0.00015 inches. Length of dermal spicules 0.00375; of gemmule spicules 0.002 inches.

This sponge in all its parts is a very slender edition of *S. lacustris* but I think deserves a varietal designation.

S. lacustris, var. **multiforis,** Carter. Ann. etc. 1881, p. 88.

I understand Mr. Carter to agree with me in now regarding this as a variety of *S. lacustris;* the multiple openings being probably the result, in degree, of over maturity. There are no distinctive features except that the skeleton spicules in the fragments sent me are unusually large.

S. lacustris, var. **lehighensis**, Potts. (Pl. VII, fig. v.)

In this variety we find the skeleton and dermal spicules normal, while those of the gemmules are disproportionately large. The gemmule itself is relatively small, with an unusually thick granular crust, through which, embedded like *chevaux de frise*, the spicules project their points, crossing their lines in every direction. These are long, cylindrical, with long spines; those near the extremities often recurved; terminations acute.

Loc. Lehigh river Pennsylvania, near White Haven.

Meas. Diameter of gemmule 0.016 inches. Skeleton spicules 0.01035 by 0.00045 inches. Length of dermal spicule 0.002; of gemmule spicule 0.004 inches.

A somewhat similar form was collected at May's Landing, New Jersey; but in this the chitinous body was very thick; the granular crust less conspicuous; the spicules fewer, larger, and less regular in position and character. (Pl. VII, fig. iv.) It may be briefly described thus:—

Sponge green, encrusting; not conspicuously branched.

Gemmules small, crust thin, enveloped in a specialized capsule of interlacing skeleton spicules.

Skeleton spicules stout, sub-fusiform, smooth, gradually pointed.

Dermal spicules rather large.

Gemmule spicules variably robust, abundantly spined; spines long, acute, retrorse.

Meas. Length of skeleton spicules 0.0105; of dermal spicules 0.0021; of gemmule spicules 0.004 inches.

Loc. May's Landing, N. J.

(3) **Spongilla (Euspongilla) rhenana**, Retzer. See "Diagnosis," p. 174, etc.

(4) **Spongilla alba**, Carter. Ann. etc. 1881 p. 88.

"Massive, spreading, sub-branched. Structure fragile, tomentose. Color whitish. Skeleton spicule curved, fusiform, gradually sharp-pointed, smooth. Flesh spicule thin, curved, fusiform, covered with spines, longest in the centre where they are vertical and obtuse. Statoblast globular; aperture infundibular; crust thick, white; composed of granular cell-structure, charged with minute thick acerates, which are curved, cylindrical, round at the ends, covered with spines (especially about the extremities where they are longest and much recurved), arranged tangentially, intercrossing each other like the lines of an engine-turned watch-case." Carter.

Loc. Bombay.

Mr. Carter observes:—"The spicules of the statoblast here as well as in *S. lacustris* are considerably stouter, more curved, cylindrical and more coarsely spined than the flesh spicules of the sponge generally."

(5) **S. cerebellata**, Bk Proc. Zool. Soc. 1863 p. 465.

Carter thinks this is but a variety of the preceding species.

(*b.*) *Sponge not branched.*

(6) **Spongilla carteri**, Bowerbank. (*S. friabilis.*) Carter. Proc. Zool. Soc. etc., 1863, p. 469.

"Sponge massive, sessile. Color greenish or faint whitish yellow; structure fragile, crumbling. Skeleton spicule smooth, fusiform, curved, gradually sharp-pointed. Statoblast globular; aperture infundibular; crust composed of pyramidal columns of dodecahedral or polyhedral cells, hexagonal in the section, regularly arranged one above another in juxtaposition, perpendicularly to the outside of the chitinous coat, on which they rest; surrounded by a layer of minute fusiform, curved and gradually sharp-pointed, smooth acerates." Carter.

Loc. Bombay, Mauritius etc.

In the spring of 1885 specimens of this sponge were kindly sent to me by Col. Nicolas Pike of Brooklyn, New York, who had collected them many years before, while United States Consul at Mauritius. He writes:—"The specimens sent you were gathered by me at the Botanical Gardens, Pamplemousses, Mauritius. They were found growing in masses five or six inches in width, three inches thick and about four in depth. They fringed the southerly side of the pond about a foot below the surface of the water. They were very green when first taken and rather firm in texture. They covered a very limited area in this pond and were not found elsewhere on the island."

The courtesy of this gentleman has enabled me to observe a peculiarity in the gemmules of his collection that was not mentioned as to those from Bombay. While many of them appear to correspond with Mr. Carter's description above:—"aperture infundibular," I find many others having a tubular prolongation of the foraminal orifice, of a length fully one fourth the diameter of the gemmule. These tubules are surrounded like the rest of the chitinous body with columns of relatively large polyhedral cells; and as they partake of the brittleness of the sponge when dry, I fancy they must often be broken off and lost in carriage.

(7) **Spongilla nitens**, Carter. Ann. etc. 1881, p. 89.

"Form of sponge unknown. Structure reticulate; fibre rigid, composed of bundles of spicules united by a transparent colorless sarcode, which, in the dried state, gives it a hardness and vitreous appearance like that of *Spongilla corallioides* Bk. Skeleton spicule curved, cylindrical, smooth, sometimes very slightly inflated in the centre and at the extremities, which are round. Statoblast globular; aperture infundibular; crust composed of pyramidal columns of dodecahedral or polyhedral cells hexagonal in the section, regularly arranged one above another, in juxtaposition, perpendicularly to the outside of the chitinous coat, on which, by the intervention of a layer of the statoblast spicules, they rest; surrounded by a layer of minute, fusiform, curved acerates, thickly spined, especially over the ends, where the spines are longest and recurved, arranged tangentially; the same kind of layer immediately round the chitinous coat, where the spicules appear to be intermixed with the lower cells of the crust, leaving the latter free between the two." Carter.

Loc. Unknown; probably South America. River Ugalla, near Lake Tanganyika, Central Africa. (See *Spongilla böhmii*.)

(8) **Spongilla navicella**, Carter. Ann. etc. 1881, p. 87.

"Sponge unknown. Skeleton spicule curved, fusiform, smooth, gradually sharp-pointed. Statoblast adherent to the twig on which the sponge had grown; globoelliptical; *aperture terminal*, infundibular; no apparent crust; chitinous coat encased with a dense layer of minute, stout, short, thick, more or less curved, fusiform, smooth acerates, variable in size, becoming so short internally, (that is where they are in immediate contact with the chitinous coat,) as to be trapezoidal or like a little boat or "cocked hat," according to direction in which they are viewed; arranged tangentially, crossing each other." Carter.

Loc. River Amazons, S. A.

To the above description by Mr. Carter I am able to add but little that is positive, excepting that so far as it goes it is most accurate. Upon a leaf connected with the twig that supports a specimen of *Parmula brownii*, var., received from Dr. Rusby, I find a dozen or more gemmules, easily identified as belonging to this species. They are sometimes entirely solitary; sometimes in groups of two to four or more of varying sizes, but without other association than the intervention of some grayish sedimentary matter that has not been proven to belong to a parent sponge. In no case do I find evidences of enveloping skeleton spicules, excepting that immediately under and around each gemmule it is seen to be buttressed and supported by scores of spicules of a skeleton type, resting against it at many angles, and attaching it to the supporting surface, as Mr. Carter has said. These, by the way, are obscurely microspined. The aperture of the slightly elliptical, or pro-sphæroidal gemmule, is always found at one of its poles, and is prolonged into a tubule of moderate length, provoking the comparison to a tortoise with its head protruded. The layer of gemmule-spicules is "dense" because they are not crossed but lie nearly parallel with each other as if stroked with a brush and in a nearly transverse direction, corresponding with the shorter axis of the ellipse.

The normal character of the living sponge remains, as Carter left it, an unsatisfied problem; but the absence of surrounding spicules suggests to me the possibility that the minute body of *Spongilla navicella* is simply a firmer sarcode unsupported by a skeleton framework.

(9) **Spongilla bombayensis**, Carter. Ann. etc. 1882, p. 369.

"General form of sponge unknown. Statoblast sessile, globular, more or less grouped and firmly attached to the stems of the herbaceous plant upon which it had grown; variable in size under 5/1 of an inch diameter, composed of a spiculiferous capsule, a chitinous coat, which is also spiculiferous, and the usual germinal contents, but no distinct cellular coat. Spicules of the statoblast slightly curved, thick, cylindrical, more or less obtuse at the ends; about 9 by 2-6000 ths. of an inch in greatest dimensions; and another comparatively thin, fusiform, and more or less pointed at the ends, about 10 by 1-6000 ths. inches in greatest dimensions; both thickly spined, and varying in stoutness inversely with their proximity to the surface; arranged horizontally, so that the ends do not project beyond the level of the statoblast, where they more or less cross each other and are held together by granules (the microcell structure?); appearing also in the chitinous coat when they do not cross each other but form a *single* layer, in which the spicules lie more or less parallel to each other in various directions, so as to present a damascened appearance. Skeleton spicules of one form only, viz.–acerate, curved, fusiform, gradually sharp-pointed, smooth or microspined, about 22 by 1-1800 th. inch in their greatest dimensions. Aperture of statoblast sunken, single or in plurality, lined by a tubular projection of the chitinous coat." Carter.

Loc. Island of Bombay.

(10) **Spongilla botryoides**, W. A. Haswell. Proc. Linn. Soc. N. S. Wales, 1882, p. 209.

"Sponge yellow, encrusting; skeleton spicules curved, fusiform, sparsely microspined; statoblast spicules short, strongly curved, with heads composed of numerous short, blunt or subacute spines. Shaft free from spines." Haswell.

Loc. Pond near Brisbane, Australia.

(11) **Spongilla sceptrioides.** W. A. Haswell. Proc. Linn. Soc. N. S. Wales, 1882, p. 209.

"Skeleton spicules microspined; statoblast spicules cylindrical, spined, particularly near the head."

Loc. Pond near Brisbane, Australia.

(12) **Spongilla cinerea**, Carter. Ann. and. Mag. 1881. p. 107.

"Flat, spreading; surface slightly convex, presenting gentle eminences and depressions. Color cinereous; texture compact, fine, friable. Skeleton spicule curved, fusiform, gradually sharp-pointed, minutely spined. Statoblast globular; aperture infundibular; crust thick, white, composed of microcell substance, charged with minute acerate spicules which are curved, cylindrical, abruptly sharp-pointed, and coarsely spined throughout; arranged more or less tangentially, intercrossing." Carter.

Loc. Bombay.

(13) **Spongilla fragilis**, Leidy. (Pl. V. fig. ii: Pl. VIII. figs. i, ii, iii, iv.) Proc. Acad. Nat. Sci. Phila. 1851. p. 278.

Syn.— European, See Vejdovsky, "Diagnosis." p. 176.
Syn.— American.
 1863 *S. lordii*, Bowerbank.
 1875 *S. ottawaensis*, Dawson.
 1880 *S. morgiana*, Potts.
    S. calumeti, B. W. Thomas.
 1880 *S. fragilis*, var. *minuta*, Potts.
 1880 *S. fragilis*, var. *minutissima*, Potts.
    S. fragilis, var. *irregularis*, Potts.
    S. segregata, Potts.

Sponge "discoidal, lichenoid, growing in patches flat, oval or circular, lobate at margin, translucent, yellowish white or cream colored. Areolæ distinct, subcircular. Reproductive bodies arranged in a single close layer at the base of the attachment of the sponge; shining whitish yellow, elevated into a central papilla upon the upper surface.

"*Meas.* From one half inch to two inches in diameter by one to one and a half lines in thickness at the centre and gradually thinning off to the margin.

"*Hab.* Grows upon the underside of stones below low-water mark in the rivers Delaware and Schuylkill.

"*Structure.* Composed of an intertexture of spiculæ about one four hundredth of an inch long, having a minutely tuberculated surface, over which is reflected a granulo-cellular membrane.

"*Remarks.* After the death of the sponge, the areolated tissue macerates off, leaving the reproductive bodies in a close layer attached to the rock. The living sponge is never green(?), nor does it ever grow exposed to the light."(?) Leidy.

I have thought best to preface my own description of this species as seen and collected in multitudes of localities, by the above original description by its discoverer Dr. Leidy. I append the following from my note book:—"At the Acad. Nat. Sci. January 31st. 1885—re-examined type specimen on a stone, of '*S. fragilis*, presented by J. Leidy,' taking a few spicules and statoblasts for comparison. After mounting, (Pl. VIII, fig. i,) I find the skeleton spicules average 0.0081 inches; the dermal spicules 0.0027 inches in length. One four hundredth inches as given in his description corresponds with the decimal fraction 0.0025 inches; and my measurement therefore agrees very nearly with Dr. Leidy's, of the dermal or flesh spicules. He does not describe those of the skeleton."

See further remarks as to its identification later.

I would describe it as follows:—

Sponge varying from a nearly white to a bright green according to its exposure to the light; encrusting, in subcircular patches, thin at the edges, occasionally one or more inches thick near the middle. Surface smooth or more or less tuberculated; pores and osteoles numerous; the latter sometimes one fourth inch or more in diameter at the confluence of several of the larger canals. Texture more compact than that of *S. lacustris*. (Pl. V, fig. ii.)

Gemmulæ abundant; primarily in one or more pavement layers, generally found at the base of the sponge; their foramina prolonged into tubes upon the upper or outer side; frequently curving to one side but not flaring like the funnel of a steamboat. In other positions the gemmules are found in compact groups of varying numbers; the foraminal tubules uniformly opening *outward*. (Pl. V, fig. ii, B.) In all situations they are enveloped in a parenchyma of spherical cells of nearly uniform size, made polygonal by contact, charged with multitudes of spinous acerates.

Skeleton spicules slightly curved, smooth, rather abruptly pointed. (Pl. VIII, fig. i, ii, iii, iv. a, a, a.)

True dermal spicules wanting.

Gemmule spicules or those embedded in the parenchyma, (Pl. VIII, as above, b, c. etc.) either cylindrical or larger at the middle and slightly tapering toward the extremities, which are truncate, rounded or with a single terminal spine; entirely spined; spines erect, conical or rounded; generally largest near the ends of the spicule.

Approximate measurements. Diameter of gemmules 0.02 inches. Length of skeleton spicules 0.0075 inches; of gemmule spicules 0.003 inches.

Hab. Standing or running water everywhere; rather affecting the former.

Loc. In all parts of North America heard from; Europe etc.

The proper identification of this sponge which was the first described as discovered upon the American Continent, has become a subject of particular interest on account of its recent discovery at several points in the Eastern Hemisphere. The original description by Prof. Leidy has just been quoted. It will be remarked that although the date of its publication was a dozen years prior to that of Dr. Bowerbank's "Monograph" (1863) the name does not appear in his list of species. This is explained by the absence of illustrations from Dr. Leidy's text and the unfortunate circumstance (as narrated by Dr. B. in his description of *Meyenia leidyi*,) that the sponge sent to him marked "*S. fragilis*" did not correspond with the accompanying description, but proved upon examination to belong to a novel and quite different species.

Dr. Bowerbank consequently ignored *S. fragilis* as imperfectly described and was followed by H. J. Carter in a similar omission. I take pleasure in restoring the name to its proper place in the literature of the subject, associating it with the species now described for the following reasons:—

In 1878 or 1879 my attention was first attracted to the subject of fresh-water sponges by the discovery of a few gemmules, resembling a rust-colored incrustation, upon a stone from Lansdowne Run, Philadelphia. Noticing the variation of the truncate flesh spicules from the pointed acerates in the descriptions of *S. lacustris* and *S.*

fluviatilis, then only known to me, the sponge to which they belonged was, not unreasonably perhaps, supposed to be new, and the name *Spongilla morgiana* was suggested for it, (Proc. Acad. Nat. Sci. July 1880) from a fanciful resemblance of the gemmules with their upright foramina, to the jars in which the "Forty Thieves" were so neatly "done in oils" by that consummate artist. On coming to a knowledge of Dr. Leidy's description some months later, I sought and found *this* sponge in his (Dr. L's) original localities. Repeated comparison of the sponge with the above description resulted in the conviction of their entire agreement, if we regard the author as examining a mass of sessile gemmules after the skeleton spicules had been generally removed. At last a small stone was discovered in in the museum of the Philadelphia Academy, to which was attached the legend, in the author's handwriting, "*S. fragilis* presented by J. Leidy," and still bearing a few gemmules and spicules of the same species. The identification was then complete, and *S. lordii*, Bk. 1863; *S. ottawaensis*, Dawson, 1875; and *S. morgiana*, Potts 1880, became synonyms.

Next to *S. lacustris*, *Spongilla fragilis* is the most widely distributed American species; having been found in most of the United States and in all varieties of situations. It seems to grow indifferently, in rapidly flowing streams, in currentless reservoirs, and even in nearly stagnant pools. Where it is found at all, the specimens are usually abundant. Upon one occasion when the water was withdrawn from the canal basin at the head of the locks at Fairmount Dam, Philadelphia, the exposed, perpendicular walls of dressed stone were seen to be lined with them, probably hundreds in number; some of minute size, but many covering two or three square feet of surface. They were rarely much more than an inch thick near the middle and shaded off all around to filmy edges. They had no apparent preference for the comparatively rough surface of the stones, for some of the finest specimens were found upon the timbers of the gates, from which they were easily removed.

The large size of the efferent osteoles in this species is a conspicuous feature; and within each of them can be seen the terminations of five or six of the larger canals. When mature, say in August or later, the pavement layer of gemmules may generally be found at the base of such specimens; and in those still older, the segregate or grouped forms are frequently abundant in the higher parts of the sponge.

These *groups* were not observed or described by Dr. Leidy, and
when first noticed by myself were supposed to indicate either a
new species or variety; but it was long ago discoverd that to a
greater or less extent they formed a characteristic feature of *all types*
of *Spongilla fragilis*. It has seemed to me that while the "pavement
layer" of gemmules was firmly attached to its base of support, indicating a purpose to reproduce the sponge at the *same* place, the
groups, which are not so attached, and are liberated by the slough-
ing away of the skeleton spicules during the winter season, float
off and serve to propagate the species in *distant localities*. They
must not be understood to be merely accidental collections of gemmules in the same neighborhood and without coherence, (as is the
case with those of *S. aspinosa*); but to be closely and permanently
associated and embedded in a mass of compact "cell-structure"; (the
"cellular crust" of Carter, the "external parenchyma" of Vejdovsky);
sometimes but three or four together, (Pl. V, fig. ii, B.) compared
by H. J. Carter to the tetraspores of *Selaginella*;—sometimes a doz-
en or more, very irregularly grouped, but *always* with their foraminal tubules projecting *outward* through the crust; in which vast
numbers of spined spicules are embedded.

The spicules of this class are very variable in shape in the different localities in which this species has been found; being long or
short; robust or slender; truncate or pointed; while the *general*
characteristics of the species remain unquestionable. A few varieties that appear constant have been named. Upon nearly every
slide of prepared gemmules or spicules may be seen a few abnormal,
spherical forms, bristling with spines, and reminding one of the pol-
len of Malvaceous plants, or the "caltrops" in sometime military
use.

S. fragilis, (*S. lordii*, Bowerbank.) Syn. Proc. Zool. Soc. 1863.

Dr. Bowerbank's description is here copied for convenient reference. The species would have been "good" in his name had it not
been antedated twelve years, by Dr. Leidy.

"Sponge sessile, coating; surface even, smooth. Osculæ simple,
dispersed. Pores inconspicuous. Dermal membrane pellucid,
aspiculous. Skeleton spicula acerate. Ovaria congregated on the
basal membrane, very numerous; spicula entirely spined, fusiform-
cylindrical, dispersed on the surface. Basal membrane abundantly
spiculous; spicula dispersed, same as those of the ovaries. Color
ochreous yellow to green."

Spongilla fragilis, (*S. segregata*, Potts.) Syn.

My error in separating this form has been acknowledged.

S. fragilis, (*S. calumeti*, Thomas.) Syn.

This form has very robust gemmule spicules. (Pl. VIII, fig. iii.)

S. fragilis, var. **minuta,** Potts. (Pl. VIII, fig. iv.) Proc. Acad. Nat. Sci. 1880 p. 357.

This varietal name was given to a sponge first found at Lehigh Gap, Pennsylvania, in which the gemmules were much smaller than in the typical form, while the surrounding spicules were nearly double the length of those of the same class in it and were nearly always terminated by a single sharp spine. It has since been found at several other localities.

Meas. Skeleton spicules 0.01 by 0.0004 inches. Gemmule spicules 0.00463 by 0.00025 inches.

S. fragilis, var. **minutissima,** Potts. (Pl. VIII, fig. ii.)

The gemmules of var. *minutissima* are still smaller than those of var. *minuta*; the groups consist of greater numbers of individuals; the cell-structure surrounding them is still coarser and more conspicuous. The skeleton spicules of those collected in Lake Hopatcong, New Jersey, (alt. 1200 ft. above tide.) are very slender and although gathered in October often centrally inflated.

Meas. Skeleton spicules 0.0064 by 0.00015 inches; gemmule do. 0.00397 by 0.0001 inches.

S. fragilis, v. irregularis, Potts.

In this, which was also collected at Lake Hopatcong, the skeleton spicules are short and slender; gemmule spicules irregularly bent and inflated.

Meas. Length of skeleton spicules 0.0042 inches; of gemmule do. 0.003 inches.

(14) **Spongilla igloviformis,** Potts. n. sp. (Pl. V, fig. iii. Pl. VIII, fig. v.)

Sponge light or dark brown, encrusting, thin; surface somewhat corrugated, or smooth, excepting the projecting points of spicules. Lines of skeleton spicules much dispersed, forming no recognizable intertexture; the sarcode in this species being at its maximum, in relation to the skeleton spicules, which are seen at their minimum as to numbers.

Gemmules very numerous, in compact groups of eight or ten to twenty or more; irregularly disposed upon, but not attached to, the supporting surface. These groups are approximately hemispherical in shape, resting upon a flat subcircular side or base, above which they form a dome-shaped mass suggesting a resemblance to the *igloe* or hut of an Eskimo (Pl. V, fig. iii, A.). The foraminal apertures of the gemmules composing these groups, contrary to their uniform habit in *S. fragilis*, *all open inward*, apparently communicating with a central cavity within the mass or group. Each gemmule, as in the last named species, is enveloped in a cellular parenchyma, which also, by short isthmus-like bands, connects it with the adjoining gemmules and finally compacts the members of a group together; but, whereas the parenchymal cells of *S. fragilis* are nearly uniform in size, these are very variable, being large upon the superfices of the gemmule proper and upon the outer surface of the envelope; while the interior cell-structure is with difficulty resolvable under a one-fifth objective. This parenchyma is densely charged with echinating spicules.

Skeleton spicules very few, sub-fusiform, but somewhat enlarged *near* the terminations, then abruptly pointed or rounded; sparsely microspined; spines short, obtuse. (Pl. VIII, fig. v, a.a.)

Gemmule spicules exceedingly numerous, nearly as long as those of the skeleton; sub-fusiform, abruptly pointed, entirely spined. Spines long, acute; perpendicular at the middle of the spicules while those near either end are strongly recurved. (Pl. VIII, fig. v, b.b.)

Meas. Skeleton spicules 0.0099 by 0.0004 inches; gemmule spicules 0.00657 by 0.0004 inches.

Hab. Upon the lower side of timbers etc. in Cedar swamps near the East coast of New Jersey.

Loc. Collected as yet only near Absecum and Vineland N. J.

The points of difference between this species and *S. fragilis* seem obvious. I find them in the spinous character of the skeleton spicules; in the want of fibrous structure in the sponge itself; in the different characters of the gemmule spicules; in the absence of a pavement layer of gemmules; in the peculiar flat-sided arrangement of the groups and in the fact that the germinal apertures all open inward.

This sponge was discovered during a memorable visit to Doughty's Pond, Absecum, New Jersey, December 1st. 1883. The locality has been described in the general remarks under the head of *Spongilla aspinosa*. Just before leaving the place, happening to draw up a submerged slab lying in shallow water near the saw-mill, I found, irregularly scattered upon its under side, a quantity of large, light-colored particles, disconnected from any noticeable sponge growth, and looking suspiciously like large grains of sawdust. They were so much larger than ordinary statoblasts, that, not delaying to examine them minutely, I filled one or two bottles on "general principles" merely and took them with me. My pleasure in examining them after reaching home and chagrin at the recollection that, contrary to my usual custom, I had left the slab half drawn out of the water, was such that I wrote by the next mail to the proprietor of the mill, requesting him to restore the timber with the remaining embryos to their native element. On two subsequent visits I was successful in finding and collecting growing sponges of this species, exhibiting the peculiarities described in the technical part of this description.

From a somewhat similar pond in the neighborhood of Vineland N. J. my friend U. C. Smith Esq. has, on two occasions, brought me gemmules of the same species.

From MacKay's Lake, near Pictou, Nova Scotia, Mr. A. H. MacKay has kindly sent what seems to me the same or a nearly related species, which was described a year later by Mr. Carter under the name of

(15) **Spongilla mackayi**, Carter. Ann. and Mag. Jan. 1885, p. 19.

"Sponge sessile, spreading; charged with little sub-globular bodies, like large statoblasts, about one twelfth inch in diameter. Skeleton spicules acerate, slightly curved, sharp-pointed, more or less thickly spined; averaging 50 by 2½–6000ths. inches in their greatest dimensions. Statoblast globular, consisting of a thick chitinous coat filled with the usual germinal matter, from which is very slightly prolonged an everted trumpet-shaped aperture; bearing slight traces externally of microcell-structure and the polygonal tissue; making one of twenty such which are so arranged as to form a sub-globular body of the size mentioned; situated around a central cavity with their apertures *inwards*; the whole supported by statoblast spicules of various sizes, which, intercrossing each other form a nest-like globular capsule in which the outer parts of the statoblasts are fixed and covered; apparently, (for the specimen is dry) deficient at one point, which leads into the central cavity. Statoblast spicules acerate, sharp-pointed like the skeletal spicules, but becoming much shorter and more coarsely spined as they approach the chitinous coats of the statoblasts, where they may be reduced to at least $\frac{27}{5000}$ ths. inches in length, although often increased to $\frac{1}{5000}$ ths. inches in thickness, and their spines, which are very irregular in size and situation, often as long as the spicule is broad." Carter.

Loc. MacKay's Lake, near Pictou, Nova Scotia.

(16) **Spongilla böhmii**, Hilgendorf. Ann. and Mag. N. H. Vol. XII, 1883. p. 122.

"Sponge parasitic upon masses of *Spongilla nitens*, appearing as an inconspicuous crust of only one millimetre in thickness; consisting of a very fine-meshed, delicate frame work. The magnificent gemmulæ are grouped in a single layer of from 8 to 12 within the skeleton, but at the same time much projecting from it; always very few in number.

"A delicate homogeneous lamella sharply divides the two species.

"The skeleton spicules are similar in form to those of *S. nitens*, but are only half their length, and instead of being smooth are studded with roundish, flattened tubercles, which at the ends approach considerably closer together.

"They are accompanied by a four times smaller amphidiscoid form, whose shaft is gently curved and bears at some distance from the the centre a small spherical elevation. From a similar one at each end of the shaft proceeds five short, pointed, recurved prongs, exactly as in a whorl. These double whorls lie close to the large spicules and form with them the network, the threads, of which are mostly but one spicule in thickness.

"The gemmulæ have not the layer of parenchyma; the spicules lie tangentially and in only a single layer; but they are densely crowded and at the same time minute; so that their number is very considerable and may exceed a thousand in one gemmule. Each spicule is moderately curved, cylindrical, with only the last eighth or tenth tapering to a point. The surface bears a moderate number of short acute spines; say 50 on the entire spicule." Slightly abbreviated from M. Hilgendorf.

Loc. River Ugalla near Lake Tanganyika, Central Africa; collected by Dr. R. Böhm.

Through the good offices of my friend Mr. Carter and the kindness of Dr. Weltner, of Berlin, I have been favored to receive from Dr. Hilgendorf of the Berlin Zool. Museum, where it was deposited, an excellent specimen of *S. nitens*, bearing upon one of its surfaces a film of the above *S. böhmii*, ample for comparison with the next species, *S. novæ terræ*, which, in one point, it most curiously resembles. Having given above the very clear description by Dr. M. Hilgendorf, it is needful only to explain that while *such* a "layer of parenchyma" around the gemmule as that seen in its associate species, *S. nitens*, is absent, the gemmule of *S. böhmii* is provided with a thick "granular crust" beneath which the gemmule spicules are embedded, a capsule of skeleton spicules enveloping the whole. The dermal or flesh spicules, as he describes them, are minute *birotulates*, nearly resembling those of *S. novæ terræ* and *Meyenia everetti*, but somewhat larger than either; the shafts are more frequently bent and a bolder enlargement at each extremity gives origin to more widely spreading hooked rays. I incline to the opinion that the occasional inflations of the shafts of these spicules as well as of the spicules of the gemmule, indicate a want of full maturity in the specimen when gathered.

My interest in the description given of this little species by Dr. Hilgendorf was such as to induce me to ask, through Mr. Carter, the opportunity of making a personal examination of it; more particularly, to discover whether in it, as in *S. novæ terræ*, the birotulate dermal was associated with a gemmule acerate showing any tendency toward a birotulate form. This I find is no more the case than in several other species of *Spongilla*; *S. fragilis* for instance, where there is also a grouping of recurved rays *near* the extremities.

The curious fact that a coincidence of type has here associated the Island of Newfoundland with Central Africa, will not escape the notice of any one; nor that a corresponding form in a neighboring genus should only appear, as yet, in places so remote as a corner of Massachusetts and the Lakes of Nova Scotia.

(17) **Spongilla novæ terræ**, Potts. Proc. Acad. Nat. Sci. Phila. 1881, p. 228 etc.

Sponge encrusting; sarcode of the young growth, a dense mass of minute spherical cells, embedding slender, curving lines of fasciculated skeleton spicules, developing later into a very loose, open tissue, with few connecting spicules.

Gemmules rather numerous, unusually large, spherical; chitinous coat thin; crust apparently wanting.

Skeleton spicules relatively few, slender, cylindrical, smooth or sparsely microspined; gradually pointed. (See cut.)

Dermal or flesh spicules very abundant, minute *birotulates* of unequal size; shafts slender, cylindrical, occasionally spined; outer surface of rotules dome-shaped; rays prolonged, terminations acute; malformations frequent. These are mixed with occasional linear spined spicules.

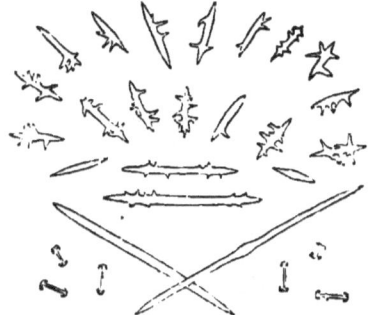

Gemmule spicules abundant, crossing each other upon the crustless, chitinous body. Their shape when smooth is robust-fusiform, with pointed terminations: the great majority, however, have from one to six or more long spines, non-symmetrically placed, but with an evident tendency to group themselves at points about one-fourth the length of the spicule from one or both of its extremities.

Meas. Diameter of gemmules 0.036 inches; skeleton spicules 0.0068 by 0.0002 inches; length of average dermal birotulate, 0.00066 inches; and of those of the gemmule 0.00145 inches.

Hab. Encrusting stones in shallow water.

Loc. Lakes or ponds in the vicinity of Heart's Content, Newfoundland; collected by Mr. A. H. MacKay.

As the unusual features of this sponge give it a peculiar importance, I am tempted to copy the results of an entirely independent study of it by my friend Mr. Carter, taken from a letter written to the discoverer, Mr. MacKay. The comparison of it with that above given may be both interesting and instructive, as showing how the same peculiarities, equally new to both, may impress different observers.

"Specimen sessile, spreading over two sides of a cubic stone about two inches in diameter; about one sixth inch high in the center, thinning off towards the circumference. Color of the surface greenish; of the interior greyish brown. Surface smooth, shining, (in the dried state), covering a parenchymatous structure beneath, traversed by thread-like bundles of the skeletal spicules of the species, charged with statoblasts.

Statoblasts globular, of different sizes, but comparatively large generally; being often $\frac{235}{6000}$ths of an inch in diameter; covered in a tessellated manner, by a single layer of short fusiform spicules in juxtaposition and all on the same level.

Fusiform spicule short, thick and smooth fundamentally, averaging 10 by 1-6000th. inch in its greatest dimensions, but variable in length, presenting one to twelve spines most whimsically scattered over the surface, so that no two spicules are alike in this respect. Aperture of the statoblast single, circular, slightly marginated, about $\frac{5}{5000}$ths. inch in diameter.

Skeletal spicule slightly curved, smooth and gradually pointed comparatively small, forming, by overlapping each other linearly, the thread-like bundles mentioned; about 40 by 1-6000ths. inch in its greatest dimensions,

Dermal layer and tissue generally abundantly charged with minute birotulates, almost identical with those of *Meyenia everetti*, but a little larger and with longer and more recurved teeth at the terminations: about $\frac{5}{5000}$ths. inch in length."

Loc. Heart's Content, Avalon Peninsula, Newfoundland.

All the specimens of this sponge came from the neighborhood of Heart's Content, but whether they were gathered from a lake upon the heights or from a brook, mentioned by Mr. Mackay, near the sea level, does not seem entirely clear. The accompanying illustration, magnified 225 diameters will suggest the peculiarities of its skeleton (crossed below), dermal (at lower corners) and gemmular spiculation (above). The striking resemblance (alluded to by Mr. Carter), of the dermal spicules to the minute birotulates, heretofore only known in a corresponding position, in the cases of *Meyenia everetti* and *Spongilla böhmii*, will at once impress the student. These are however more variable in size, are occasionally spined, and have their rays more prolonged and more delicately terminated.

It is in the singular character of the spicules surrounding the gemmules that this species must attract peculiar attention. As the reader must already have discovered, the six genera included in Carter's system may be divided into two principal groups; one of them including only the genus *Spongilla*, characterized by the *linear*, *acerate* spicules surrounding the gemmules; and the other, comprising all the other genera, where the spicule of corresponding significance is a *birotulate* or some easily recognized derivative of that type. Within this latter and larger group, intermediate forms, connecting the defined genera, are frequent, and the location of species upon one side or other of the distinctive line, comparatively unimportant. Heretofore, between the genus *Spongilla* and those genera comprised in the other group there has been "a great gulf fixed." One only case in the past has suggested their possible association, or the development of one group from the other.

By referring to the description of *Meyenia fluviatilis*, var *acuminata*, mihi, it will be seen, that in that variety, the shafts of the birotulates are prolonged at each extremity, forming acuminate terminations some distance beyond the surface of the rotules. It must be noticed also, that in position these spicules are abnormal, lying flat upon the chitinous coat, instead of resting upon one rotule, their shafts taking the position of radii, as is usual in this genus. We have here in fact spicules of a *Meyenia* occupying the ordinary positions, and in degree approximating the forms of those regarded as peculiar to the *Spongillæ*.

In the present species the intermediate character of the gemmule-spicules is still more striking; and while their form and position probably more closely associate them with the genus *Spongilla*, in which I have, after considerable hesitation, placed the species, the grouping of ray like spines is forcibly suggestive of *Meyenia*; it will be therefore no cause for surprise, if further examination shall cause its transfer to the sister genus.

It must not escape notice that in both of these instances the gemmulæ are without "crust," and as it is difficult to understand how birotulates could be supported in their *ordinary* positions without these embedding granules, we may not unreasonably infer a possible relation of cause and effect between the change in position, and the modification of type that we here find.

As this is the first novel species of fresh water sponge collected upon the Island of Newfoundland, as also, this is the highest latitude in North America from which any collections have been recorded, it may be well to append to the above, in which the original report to the Proc. Acad. Nat. Sci. (1886) has been closely followed, the remarks of Mr. MacKay, as to the extremes of temperature etc. in that region.

He says: "The Island is not extreme in its temperature, and the frost does not go very deep into the soil. The lakes freeze in November or December with ice at least a foot in thickness, and remain closed until the end of April. The average temperature during eight years, from 1857 to 1864, was 41.2° Fahr.; average maximum thermometer during the same time 83°; minimum, 7°. In the year 1879, the mean temperature was 40.2° Fahr; highest record, August 3rd, 82°; lowest, December 22, +4°. In Nova Scotia, though that is so much further south, the range is far greater, from 96° to —20° or —24° Fahr.; with an annual average of 44°."

(II) Gen. MEYENIA, Carter, Ann. and Mag. etc. 1881, p. 90.

Gen. Char. Skeleton spicules acerate, curved, fusiform, pointed or rounded, smooth or variably spined. Gemmules globular or oval, enveloped in a granular crust, charged with birotulate spicules (Pl. IX, b. b. etc.) of a single class or type, radially arranged; *i. e.* with one rotule resting upon or approximating to the chitinous coat, the shaft erect and the other rotule forming, or projecting beyond the surface of the gemmules. (Pl. V fig. v and vi.)

The existence of birotulate spicula (then called amphidisks) in the crust surrounding the gemmule of some sponges was first pointed out by F. J. F. Meyen, (1839) who made them the distinctive characteristics of *Spongilla fluviatilis*; thus distinguishing that species from *S. lacustris*, with which until that time it had been constantly confused. In his generic revision of the group, finding that several species possessed the same peculiarity, Mr. Carter, with excellent taste, grouped under the name of Meyen those that exhibited this feature in its simplest conditions.

Next to *Spongilla* in importance, as it follows it in our classification, the genus *Meyenia* appears to be the most widely diffused throughout the world; and its leading species, *M. fluviatilis*, like *S. lacustris* is found exhibiting many variations, to perplex the student and tempt him to the creation of unnecessary names. The following is presented as a guide to the approximate determination of the several species.

KEY TO THE SPECIES OF THE GENUS MEYENIA.

(*a*) *Margins of birotulate spicules entire.*

1. Skeleton spicules covered with powerful spines. Spool-like birotulates upon the surface of the gemmulæ covered with a deep parenchyma of large cells.

Meyenia, (*Trochospongilla*) *erenaceus.*

2. Skeleton spicules *smooth*, short, robust; margins of short birotulates *exflected*; each gemmule enclosed in a capsule of skeleton spicules. (Pl. V fig. iv, Pl. X, fig. i.) *M. leidyi.*

3. Rotulæ *large, flat*; gemmules furnished with an envelope charged with *spined spicules.* *M. gregaria.*

4. Gemmules about one fourth the size of those of other species.

M. minuta.

(b) *Margins of birotulate spicules rayed.*

5. Skeleton spicules either smooth or microspined; dermals wanting; birotulates short, shafts generally smooth; margins of rotules irregularly rayed. (Pl. V fig. v; Pl. IX figs. i, to iv.)
M. fluviatilis.

6. Birotulates in two or three series. *M. (Ephydatia) mülleri.* (See also genus *Pleiomeyenia.*)

7. Parasitic on *S. lacustris*; foramina funnel shaped.
M. bohemica.

8. Birotulate spicules generally malformed; shafts with enormous spines, etc. (Pl. IX fig. v.) *M. robusta.*

9. Birotulates rather long, shafts smooth; margins of rotules lacinulate. (Pl. X fig. ii.) *M. mitlsii.*

10. Rays and spines of birotulates subdivided or microspined. (Pl. IX fig. vi.) *M. subdivisa.*

11. Dermal spicules with long, erect spines; birotulates long, spined; rays incurved. *M. baileyi.*

12. Birotulates rather long; margins crenulate or granular.
M. capewelli.

13. Gemmules flask-shaped; apertures terminal; birotulates very short, obscure. *M. anonyma.*

14. Shafts of birotulates much spined. *M. ramsayi.*

15. Birotulates many times longer than the diameter of the hooked rotules; shafts spiniferous. (Pl. V, fig. vi. Pl. X, fig. v.)
M. crateriformis.

16. Gemmule birotulates long, club-like. Dermal spicules also *birotulate*, minute. (Pl. X, fig. iii and iv).
M. everetti.

17. Gemmule birotulates long, spinous; margins of rotules notched; dermal spicules stellate. (Pl. X, fig. vi.) *M. plumosa.*

(*a*) *Margins of birotulate spicules entire.*

(1) **Meyenia (Trochospongilla) erenaceus,** Ehrenburg. See Vejdovsky's "Diagnosis." p. 177

In his description Prof. Vejdovsky has not, I think, invested the parenchyma surrounding the gemmule of this species with sufficient importance. From specimens which he has kindly sent to me, I am led to regard this feature, at least to this degree, as unique amongst the sponges, and I regret my inability to furnish an illustration of it. I do not know whether the sponge mass bears any external resemblance to that of *M. leidyi*, but they are unquestionably distinct species.

(2) **Meyenia leidyi,** Carter. Ann. and Mag. 1881, p. 91. (Pl. V, fig. iii. Pl. X, fig. i.)

Spongilla leidyi, Bk. (Proc. Zool. Soc. 1863, p. 445 etc.)

"Sponge sessile, coating, thin; surface tuberculated, minutely hispid; oscula numerous, small, congregated, elevated and marginated; pores conspicuous. Skeleton spicula acerate, small, short and stout, rather obtusely terminated. Dermal and interstitial membranes aspiculous. Ovaria spherical, small; dermal spicula birotulate, minute, short; shaft cylindrical; rotulæ margins entire, that of the outer one sometimes exflected and rarely spiculated."(?) Bowerbank.

The above is Dr. Bowerbank's original description after the examination of one dry specimen. During the past six years I have collected the species, scores of times and perhaps in greater quantity than any other. I will describe it as I have seen it.

Sponge of a peculiar light gray or drab color, even when exposed to the light; encrusting, thin. *Persistent;* the growths of successive seasons forming as many series of thin lamina. Surface even, sometimes rising into smooth rounded prominences, and at times covered with singular radiating or bird-track-like markings, whose cause is not fully understood. Pores and osteoles numerous, minute; the latter being found along the radiate lines, but not conspicuously at their confluence. Texture very compact; composed of short spicules, very slightly fasciculated; the primary lines and principal channels nearly perpendicular; with single intercalating spicules forming polyhedral interspaces.

Gemmules numerous, sub-spherical, deposited at the base of the sponge and, in successive seasons, in serial layers above (or below?) the first. Each mature gemmule is surrounded, outside of the birotulate armature, by a lattice work or capsule, composed of spicules resembling those of the skeleton; an open space being left at the top around the short, tubular foramen (Pl. V, fig, iii, A). When more than one of these is present, they are grouped together, and the open space of the capsule is correspondingly enlarged. Before maturity a granular crust embeds and surrounds the dense layer of short birotulates, but after the latticed capsule is formed, (at least when examined in a dry state) I have not been able to discover it.

Skeleton spicules short, smooth, robust; when mature very abruptly terminated, almost rounded. (Pl. X, fig. i, a,a,a,b,b.)

Dermal and interstitial surfaces aspiculous.

Birotulate spicules surrounding the gemmules very short, umbonate; rotules sometimes twisted or contorted; margins entire; generally exflected or turned up saucer-like, away from the surface of the gemmule; the diameter of the outer rotule generally rather less than that of the proximal one. (Pl. X, fig. i, c,d, etc.)

Meas. Skeleton spicules 0·00466 by 0·00045 inches. Length of birotulates 0·00045 inches. Diameter of large rotule 0·00055 inches, and of shaft 0·0001 inches.

Hab. Encrusting timbers and stone work at various, probably sometimes at great, depths.

Loc. Found as yet only in the Schuylkill River and reservoirs near Philadelphia; at Windmill Island in the Delaware River; and near Phillipsburg, New Jersey.

Several circumstances give to this species of fresh water sponge peculiar interest and importance. Described at first from a specimen inadvertently sent by Prof. Leidy to Dr. Bowerbank, as mentioned by the latter in his "Monograph," (Proc. Zool. Soc. 1863, p. 445) and already alluded to in my historical sketch of *Spongilla fragilis*, it appears to have remained unseen and uncollected from 1863 until 1880 when the writer rediscovered it at the original locality,—the neighborhood of Fairmount Dam on the Schuylkill River, Philadelphia. I am not aware that any has been found elsewhere, excepting at Windmill Island in the Delaware River, near by, and a single dry specimen, origin unknown, upon a stick which I picked up upon the bank, high above the Delaware River at Phillipsburg, New Jersey.

Fairmount Dam, just mentioned and frequently referred to in these pages, is, of course, already known to Philadelphians; but as it has been spoken of as one of the richest localities in the world for fresh water sponges, a brief description of the situation may be allowed, for the information of others. It is situated at the head of tide water in the Schuylkill River within the limits of the City of Philadelphia. It supplies upon one side, a system of locks pertaining to the Schuylkill Navigation Co. and on the other, pours its living floods through the magnificent turbine water wheels, by which the pumps are operated, that raise a large portion of the water-supply of the City to the subsiding and distributing reservoirs upon the summit of the neighboring Fairmount Hill. The direction of the dam breast is not at right angles to the course of the stream, but follows a line of rocks diagonally toward the northwest, turning abruptly to the southwest, when one or two hundred feet from the heavy masonry of the canal locks.

The exposed portions consist of heavy timbers and planking; the top and a lower section being horizontal or nearly so, connected by an inclined slide or shoot. To increase the depth of the water above the dam, for the benefit of the Philadelphia Water Works, a series of planks have been hinged to the upper, horizontal portion, and are retained in a perpendicular position, by inclined stays or props. When the river is full, the water stands against these and overflows them, nearly two feet above the normal level of the dam. During the summer season, however, the diminished supply is so drawn upon by the operation of the canal locks, the water works and ordinary leakage, that there is rarely any overflow for several months together. At such times it has been my custom frequently to walk from one side of the river to the other upon the horizontal timbers, examining at leisure the inner (upper) side of this planking; and my collections have principally been made from their smooth surfaces, when, illuminated by the afternoon sun, every adherent growth was easily seen through the unruffled surface of the water. Not that the stream is perennially unruffled by any means, for at its best the wave from a passing steamboat is likely to flood the unwary scientist at an unexpected moment. I only allude to this quiet hour, with the declining sun nearly in front of the explorer, as presenting the most favorable conditions for collecting. Upon a single visit, I have gathered from these timbers, specimens of *S. lacustris*, *S. fragilis*, *M. leidyi*, *M. fluviatilis* and *M. crateriformis*, with minute portions of *H. argyrosperma*. The first three may be considered permanent inhabitants of the locality, the others as occasional visitants.

In the forebay of the water works and in the reservoirs above, *M. leidyi* is very abundant, covering all standing timbers, horizontal pipes and frame work, as well as the dressed stone facings of the piers etc. In tide water in both the Schuylkill and Delaware Rivers, it is found at the greatest depth examined, say eight feet below low water, and probably grows much deeper; while most of our other sponges seem to prefer the neighborhood of the surface. In the subsiding reservoirs upon Fairmount Hill and in other places about Philadelphia, it especially affects the cribs and screens at the head of the discharge pipes. When the water has been drawn off for cleaning I have found it covering yards of surface at such places, though it rarely attained an inch in thickness. One such locality is particularly remembered,-the so-called Corinthian Avenue reservoir, which had not been emptied for several years; here the finest specimens might have been gathered, literally "by the bushel," and probably one half that measure was taken away in great slices or "slabs" under my arm.

These masses were almost certainly the results of many years undisturbed growth. I have described this species as persistent, to a degree unknown and almost impossible to imagine, in the case of any other North American sponge. The compactness of its skeleton texture is such, that, except in the event of actual violence, such as the pressure of ice etc., I do not believe that the spicules slough away during the winter, as do most of the others. Its gemmules, therefore, are rarely liberated, and the species in consequence is not largely diffused.

Transverse sections through the masses alluded to, show an upper or outer layer, about one eighth inch in thickness, of skeleton spicules in their normal positions, as formed; and below them a series of rather irregular lamina, composed almost entirely of gemmules, within their specialized lattice capsules.

The years of occasional study already given to this species leave several problems yet unanswered; prominent among which, is that of the order of these serial growths; which I must refer to my more successful followers. My difficulty may be stated thus. Let us suppose a sponge of this species, at the end of its first season's growth. It then, undoubtedly, consists of a layer of gemmules, surmounted by a film of skeleton spicules. There is reason to believe that little of the latter will be washed away during the winter season, but when spring comes, the contents of the gemmules, escaping through their foraminal orifices will probably(?) reclothe the naked skeleton (realizing Ezekiel's vision of the dry bones,) secrete fresh silica and at a slow rate continue the growth of the mass.

As the next season of hybernation arrives, what must happen? A second layer of gemmules will be deposited; but where? It does not appear to be at the summit of the sponge of the first season; for our section, in that case, would show a regular alternation of gemmules and of skeleton spicules in position. Is the second layer, then, formed above the first of the series of gemmules or below it? That is, in my fragment, now probably ten or twelve years of age, are the most recent gemmules highest or lowest in the series? I confess my inability, as yet, to answer the question. If freshness of appearance is taken as a guide, the latter seems the more probable supposition. Numbers of gemmules without capsular covering are to be found in both situations and the foraminal openings, which may be said to be generally upon the upper side, are found in some parts of the series upon the lower. The problem remains open.

The peculiar markings upon the external surface of the sponge, form another perplexing feature. Upon other sponges we see the terminations of submerged canals, partially exposed by the rupture of the thin dermal film which alone covered them; here, the markings consist of spicular ridges, sometimes slightly grooved along their summits, and terminated at their divergent extremities by inclined efferent (or afferent?) orifices. Those who are familiar with the appearance of young, living sponges of other species, will remember that the dermal film is supported upon the points of projecting spicules, at some distance above the denser mass of the sponge, which it thus "tympanizes," to use a happy expression of Mr. Carter. The vestibule thus formed in or around them, is, in *M. leidyi*, probably on account of the shortness and non-fasciculated character of its spicules, almost or entirely wanting, and its place seems to be supplied when alive by the formation along the above-mentioned ridges, of external, sub-cylindrical, convergent canals that have not been mentioned in any other species. Upon the only occasion in which I was able to experiment upon a living sponge in this condition, I was puzzled to see the particles of carmine used in feeding it, drawn through the pores into these channels and presently sucked downward into the body of the sponge, instead of being borne forward and thrown out from them through a common orifice or chimney, as is familiar in other cases. Attempting no explanation of this reversal of ordinary methods, I merely record it as an exceptional fact.

Within some fragments collected at Windmill Island, were found many subspherical masses, like large shot, each containing three or four gemmules, embedded, not in parenchymal cells, but in a dense mass of skeleton spicules. These have not been seen elsewhere.

Some question has been raised as to the presence, in parts of this species, of spined skeleton spicules. As the result of a careful examination of large numbers of specimens I may state my belief that any such appearance has been due to the accidental intrusion of skeleton spicules of *Tubella pennsylvanica*; which species has frequently been found in contact or in close proximity with the other.

A singular effect upon the spicules of this sponge, produced either by a retardation of their growth, or a hastened disintegration, was noticed (Proc. Acad. Nat. Sci. 1884, p. 184) in the case of fragments that had grown within certain old water pipes, and were, at the time of examination, strongly marked by iron rust. A central canal here occupied fully one half the width of the skeleton spicules and was open at both extremities; and the birotulates had lost their "entire" margins and appeared delicately rayed.

It may be mentioned in this connection, that this species, more frequently than any other, has been found encrusting iron water pipes; their exteriors, when they have long lain exposed to the water; and the interiors of those of large size, to a distance of some hundreds of feet from the reservoirs, where they had grown of course, in entire darkness. I have not yet succeeded in finding either the sponge *in situ*, or its detached spicules, among the concretions that occasionally entirely close the water-way of some of the smaller pipes, near the centre of our city.

(3) **Meyenia gregaria, (S. gregaria)** Bk.   Proc. Zool. Soc. etc., 1863 p. 452.

"Skeleton spicula cylindrical, stout and rather short. Ovaria furnished with an envelope, spicula of the envelope few and scattered, cylindrical, short and stout, entirely spined. Ovaria, surface even, furnished abundantly with very short birotulate spicula; rotulæ flat, margins entire, outer surface umbonate; umbo very short, slightly convex. Shaft of spiculum cylindrical, short and stout. Color in the dried state dark, lurid green." Bowerbank.

Hab. "River Amazons, on branches of trees, periodically pendant in the water; near Villa Nova."

I have been able to identify several small groups of gemmules of this species on the stem of a twig supporting a mass of *Parmula brownii*, var. from Beni River, East Bolivia. As in this situation I have been so fortunate as to find and determine positively the spicular skeleton of the sponge itself which neither Dr. Bowerbank nor H. J. Carter had done, the following is offered as a complete description. It will solve some doubts of both the former authors.

Sponge minute, encrusting, thin; surface even; orifices very numerous, large. Skeleton spicules not fasciculated, consequently no long lines of fibre, the spicules attached and crossing one another in every direction.

Gemmules ovoid, rather numerous, approximating to one another in groups of varying numbers, surrounded upon the upper side by a rather sparse capsule of skeleton spicules, which become very numerous below, particularly around the circumference, where they buttress and elevate the gemmule above the firm basal membrane of the sponge. Foraminal apertures uniformly downward. The chitinous coat is covered by a very thin crust in which a compact series of short birotulates is embedded.

Skeleton spicules cylindrical, short and rather stout, slightly and nearly uniformly bent; terminations rounded; entirely spined; spines, low-conical, acute, more conspicuous upon the outer curves of the spicules.

No dermals seen.

Gemmule spicules birotulates with entire circular margins and extremely short shafts; rotules flat.

Meas. Average length of skeleton spicule about 0·0036 inches. Diameter of rotules 0·00045 inches; height of birotulate 0·0002.

Loc. Beni river, East Bolivia; collected by Dr. H. H. Rusby.

(4) **Meyenia minuta,** n. sp.

Sponge as seen minute, encrusting, relatively compact; the spicules non-fasciculated and without definite arrangement.

Gemmules in the dried state faintly suggested by the curvatures of the upper surface of the sponge; rather numerous, spherical, very small, (about one fourth the average diameter of those of other species), a thin granular crust embedding birotulates that are no smaller than those of the three previous species.

Skeleton spicules slender, cylindrical but gradually sharp-pointed entirely spined; spines conical, acute.

Dermal or flesh spicules wanting.

Gemmule-birotulates short, shafts smooth, thinnest at the centre; rotules nearly equal; margins entire, slightly reflexed, more particularly that of the outer rotule which thus becomes cup-shaped.

Meas. Diameter of gemmules about 0·005 inches; a line of ten or twelve of its birotulates only, being found along its semi-equator.

Hab. Found encrusting a leaf belonging to the stem upon which a mass of *Parmula brownii*, var. had formed.

Loc. Collected by Dr. H. H. Rusby along a small branch of the river Beni in Eastern Bolivia, S. A. (See also *P. brownii.*)

This is the most minute mature sponge that I have ever met with. The masses, even, can hardly be said to be visible to the naked eye without a suggestive guidance; being about one sixteenth inch in diameter. The first was found, accidentally, on a mount containing another sponge and a very careful and almost despairing search was required before another was discovered. Its generic classification has been somewhat doubtful. But for its entirely abnormal gemmules and the geographical dislocation of the sponges, it might readily have been associated with the highest serial form of *Tubella pennsylvanica*; viz., that in which the rotules are most nearly equal.

For the reasons mentioned it seems best to separate them and place it in the genus *Meyenia*, where it differs noticeably from *M. gregaria*, (found upon the same stem) and from *M. leidyi*; each of which species has a capsular envelope; also from *M. crenaceous* with its unique parenchyma of oblong cells. I have therefore made it a new *conditional* species.

(b) *Margins of birotulates rayed.*

(5) **Meyenia fluviatilis,** (S. fluviatilis) Auct. (Pl. V, fig. v, Pl. IX, figs. i to iv.)

Syn. European, See Vejdovsky "Diagnosis." p. 178.
" Asiatic, 1849, *Spongilla meyeni*, Carter.
" American:—
1875 *Meyenia (Spongilla) asperima*, Dawson.
" " " *stagnalis*, "
1880 " " *astrosperma*, Potts.
" " " *polymorpha*, "
1882 " var. *acuminata*, "
1885 " " *mexicana*, "
" " " *angustibirotulata*, Carter.
" " " *gracilis*, "

"Massive, lobate. Structure friable, crumbling. Color light yellow-brown. Skeleton-spicule curved, fusiform, gradually sharp, pointed, smooth; often spined and often centrally inflated. Statoblast globular; aperture infundibular; crust thick, composed of granular or microcell substance, charged with birotulates whose umbonate disks are deeply and irregularly denticulated, arranged parallel to each other and perpendicular to the chitinous coat." Carter. (Ann. and Mag. 1881 p. 92.)

My observations upon this species as found abundantly in all parts of North America, and in very variable forms, may be summed up as follows.—

Sponge sessile, massive, rarely throwing out short branches an inch or less in length. Color varying from light yellow or brown to a light green, according to exposure. Surface tuberculated or irregular; often exhibiting the deep grooves of incomplete, concentrating canals, covered only by the dermal film. Pores and osteoles conspicuous. Texture rather firm; main lines of skeleton spicules and of canals horizontal or nearly parallel to the base of support. Spicules fasciculated.

Gemmules numerous throughout the entire sponge, but in the deeper parts, most abundant; spherical, very variable in size; crust variable in thickness; in some forms nearly or quite wanting, whilst in others it is so thick as to promote the formation of birotulates in two or three concentric zones.

Skeleton spicules curved, fusiform, gradually pointed; varying even in the same specimen from altogether smooth to entirely spined; but nearly always smooth at the extremities; spines, when present, minute, conical. (Pl. IX, figs. i to iv.)

Dermal and interstitial spicules wanting.

Birotulate spicules of the gemmules generally short; rotules flat, irregularly rayed, occasionally microspined, rays straight, deeply cut, nearly to the centre of the rotules; shafts rarely spinous; spines long, tapering. (Pl. IX, figs. i to iv.)

Meas. Skeleton spicules 0·01 by 0·0005 inches. Length of birotulate 0·0005 inches. Diameter of rotules 0·0007 inches.

Hab. In lakes or ponds; preferring standing water.

Loc. Throughout the Eastern and Middle United States generally.

This species under its former name of *Spongilla fluviatilis* has long been known as one of the two fresh water sponges which, until recently, were the only ones generally recognized in Europe. Like *S. lacustris* it is cosmopolitan in habit, and the study of it in this country from a great number of localities, has shown that it, also, is very variable in some of its parts. For instance, its skeleton spicules, as stated above, vary, in specimens from different localities, and to a less extent in those from the same locality, or even in the same specimen, from totally smooth to entirely spined; and the species named on account of the prevalence of one or other of these conditions will have to be given up. Its birotulates also vary greatly in size and proportions, in contour of their shafts and the character of their rays. A few forms may be so definite in their peculiarities, and repeat them in so many localities, as to warrant the use of varietal names; but in this as in other cases it seems best to include all within a definite range in the species under its familiar name.

M. fluviatilis certainly cannot be called a branching sponge, but in some localities, particularly when growing on the lower side of timbers etc. or in a rapid current, I have found it bearing inconsequent processes about an inch in length. In color it inclines to a light brown or yellowish, but in our clear northern lakes, where it grows in large patches exposed upon the upper surface of stones, it is described as of a vivid green.

Meyenia fluviatilis, var. meyeni.

Spongilla meyeni, Carter.

Skeleton spicules sparsely microspined, long, cylindrical. Gemmules spherical; chitinous coat and granular crust relatively thick. Birotulates often in two or three partial series; shafts long, cylindrical, generally smooth; rays of the rotules long, conical, deeply divided. An occasional spicule may be found of an intermediate character between the acerates and the birotulates;—that is, it resembles a short acerate with whorls of short spines about one fourth its length from either end.

In his Monograph of 1881 Mr. Carter dropped this one of his original species of Bombay sponges from his classification, merging it with *M. fluviatilis*. For several reasons I incline to retain it as a variety of that species. The size of the birotulates is far greater than the average in the typical species, and their cylindrical shafts and symmetrical forms give them a peculiar beauty. Their occasional arrangement in multiple series is not unique, but the habit was first noticed in this variety.

Meas. Skeleton spicules 0·0108 by 0·0004 inches. Length of average birotulate 0·0013 inches. Diameter of rotule 0·001 inches.

M. fluviatilis, form *astrosperma*, Potts, Syn. Proc. Acad. etc. 1880, p. 357.

The name "star seeded" was applied before the author had the opportunity to compare this with the European type, or even with collections from other parts of this country. It is a beautiful form of the species, with birotulates sufficiently scattered over the surface of the gemmule, to show as stars upon a silver dome (Pl. V. fig. v.) It was found at Lehigh Gap, Pennsylvania; but cannot claim to be even a variety.

M. polymorpha, Syn. was suggested to me by the great numbers of misshapen or incomplete forms surrounding the statoblasts; as in (Pl. IX, fig. iv, e, c, e.) These, as my friend Mr. Carter has shown me, are nearly all abortive birotulates; and when we inquire into their cause we find that they occur almost solely upon gemmules where the granular crust is wanting. How this absence so affects them, and, in fact, how this class of spicules is developed upon the chitinous coat, must be left to the investigations of later students.

The abnormal habit just mentioned leads us to consider the next variety, in which the modification assumes greater definiteness.

M. fluviatilis var. acuminata, Potts. (Pl. IX. fig. ii.) Proc. Acad. Nat. Sci. 1882, p. 70.

"Sponge probably altogether sessile and massive, consisting of an intertexture of stout, fusiform-acerate skeleton spicules, abruptly pointed, coarsely spined, except near the extremities; spines subconical, acute, dermal spicules absent or undiscovered. Gemmules without granular crust; some of them supporting a few, misplaced, irregular or malformed birotulate spicules, the distinguishing feature of which, is the prolongation of the familiar boss or umbo upon the outer surface of each rotule, into a long, acuminate spine, in line with and a continuation of the shaft."

Meas. Skeleton spicules 0·00985 by 0·0005 inches. Length of birotulates 0·00107 inches. Diameter of rotules 0·0007 inches.

To the description above quoted from the "Proceedings etc.," is appended the following in regard to the association of this variety of *M. fluviatilis* with *Spongilla* var. *paupercula* in the Boston Water supply.—

"The exceptional features referred to as marking this collection of sponges, were; first, the fact that all the gemmules, whether belonging to the genus *Spongilla* or *Meyenia*, were *smooth*, that is without a granular or cellular crust; second, the apparent absence of dermal spicules from both, and the abnormal character of those belonging to the gemmules. The occurrence of naked gemmules is not infrequent, but has, so far as known, heretofore been limited to the genus *Spongilla*. The discovery of the same feature in the associated genus *Meyenia*, coupled with the fact that of the small number of birotulates found upon them, a large proportion were imperfect, the rays being more or less aborted, approximating their shape to that of the spined, fusiform acerates of *Spongilla*, gave rise to the suggestion that here, possibly, had been not merely a mechanical mixture, by inter-, or super-position of two dissimilar species, but an organic hybridization, produced by the flowing together of the amœboid particles of which the sponge flesh is composed."

Meyenia fluviatilis, var. **mexicana,** Potts. Am. Nat. Aug. 1885, p. 810.

I find little of novelty in my description of this variety except the following. "Birotulate spicules pertaining to the gemmules, in length about three times the diameter of the rotules; shafts nearly cylindrical, sometimes more slender near the middle, irregularly spined; spines long, acute. Rotules flat, deeply notched; rays irregular, acute."

"*Meas.* Skeleton spicules 0·0152 by 0·0006 inches. Length of birotulates 0·0021 inches. Diameter of rotules 0.0009 inches."

It is added that "this species (var.) collected by Prof. E. D. Cope in Lake Xochimilco, about eight miles south of the city of Mexico, differs from the familiar *M. fluviatilis* chiefly in the far greater length of the shafts of the birotulate spicules. The specimens examined were probably collected in an immature condition, as suggested by the abundance of sarcode and the scarcity of gemmulæ or statoblasts. The single small group that alone rewarded a careful search through the whole mass of material sufficed, however, to fix its generic and approximately its specific relations. The shapes or proportions of the birotulate spicules would probably indicate its association with the following.

Meyenia fluviatilis, var. **augustibirotulata,** Carter. Ann. and Mag. etc., June 1885, p. 454.

"Sponge coating the stems of aquatic plants to the extent of one sixth of an inch in thickness all around. Consistence elastic, fragile. Color light yellow-brown. Skeletal spicule smooth, curved, fusiform, gradually sharp-pointed, varying in size under 75 by 3-6000 ths. inches in its greatest dimensions.

Statoblast globular, even on the surface, and white in color when fully developed; infundibularly depressed, over the hilous opening of the chitinous coat; about $\frac{33}{1000}$ ths. inches in diameter; consisting of the usual germinal contents, surrounded by a layer of birotules in juxtaposition, arranged perpendicularly over the chitinous coat, and filled in between with a microcell-structure up to the umbos of the birotulates, which, being naked and allowing the light to pass through them, present a dark point respectively, like minute holes in the midst of the white microcell-substance; birotule consisting of a cylindrical shaft, more or less constricted in the middle, which is sometimes furnished with one or more spines; rotule fringed toward the margin rather than denticulated, so as to present a striated appearance, which does not reach the umbo or centre; total length of birotule about $\frac{6}{1000}$ ths. inches." Carter.

Loc. England and America.

Collected by Mr. B. W. Thomas from Calumet River, near Chicago, Illinois; also by Mr. J. G. Waller, "Ditchley's Manor," Essex, England.

Meyenia fluviatilis, var. **gracilis**, Carter. Ann. and Mag. Sept. 1885, p. 180.

"Sponge delicate in structure, which is soft, whitish or colorless in spirit, presenting the aspect of glue or sarcode when dry; growing over the stem of an aquatic plant in a thin layer charged beneath with statoblasts (gemmules). Spicules of two forms, viz:—
1, skeletal, very fine and delicate, acerate, curved, cylindrical, about 34 to 36 by $\frac{1}{4}$–6000th. inch in its greatest dimensions; chiefly confined to the fibre; 2, statoblast spicules, shaft long, cylindrical, often slightly curved, smooth, also very thin and delicate; head small, flat, radiately denticulated, the ends of the rays not recurved; often umbonated by a projecting spine or process; total length about $\frac{5}{6000}$ths. inches; head $1\frac{1}{2}$–6000ths. inches in diameter; shaft about five times longer than the diameter of the head, about $\frac{1}{4}$–6000th. inch thick; chiefly confined to the statoblast, but also loose and numerous in the tissue generally. Statoblast globular when wet, hemispherical and depressed in the direction of the aperture when dry; when fully formed about 65 to 75–6000ths. inches in diameter. Aperture slightly marginated, *i. e.* slightly raised above the common level, about $\frac{5}{6000}$ths. inches in diameter. Surface of statoblast rough or uneven. In a section through the centre the crust is seen to be a little thicker than the length of the birotules, which, as usual, are arranged perpendicularly to the yellow chitinous coat beneath and parallel to each other, with one head resting on the chitinous coat and the surface of the other free at the circumference; cemented together and held in position by the microcell-structure or "float," which, projecting above the level of the outer heads of the birotules, gives rise to the roughened state of the surface of the statoblast. Chitinous coat and germinal contents the same as in the *Spongillæ* generally. Size of specimen sent to me about 1 by 1 inch horizontally." Carter.

Loc. "Ice Factory Lakes, DeLand, Florida, near the St. John's River." Collected by H. Mills.

(6) **Meyenia (Ephydatia) mülleri**, Lieberkühn. See Vejdovsky "Diagnosis." p. 177.

Of the varieties of this species v. *amphizona* and v. *mirabilis* as well as those species which Mr. H. Mills has grouped under the generic name "*Pleiomeyenia*" as *P. calumeticus*, *P. walkeri*, and *P. spinifera*, I can only say that they have been founded upon the presence of duplicate or triplicate series of birotulates around the gemmule; that this feature was observed long ago, in the case of *S. meyeni*, Carter, since merged with *Meyenia fluviatilis* by the author; and that it did not seem to him nor does it appear to me to be specific, though well worthy of notice. It may be questioned whether the peculiarity would not be found in any specimens that had grown where food or silica had been unusually abundant.

(7) **Meyenia (Ephydatia) bohemica**, F. Petr. See "Diagnosis." p. 179.

(8) **Meyenia robusta**, Potts. (Pl. IX, fig. v.)

Sponge massive, encrusting. Skeleton spicules subfusiform, pointed, smooth. Gemmules scarce, birotulates of large size and generally "monstrous" in form; irregularly shaped, shafts abounding in spines as long as the rays of the rotulæ, cylindrical or conical.

A large specimen of this species, if it be not properly a variety of *M. fluviatilis*, was found in the Museum of the Academy of Nat. Sci. of Phila. marked, "presented by Dr. Geo. H. Horn; collected by him from Honey Lake Valley near Susanville, California."

Meas. Skeleton spicules 0·01175 by 0·00055 inches. Length of birotulates 0·00095 inches. Diameter of rotules 0·0008 inches.

(9) **Meyenia millsii**. Potts. (Pl. X, fig. ii.)

Sponge encrusting; texture loose.

Gemmulæ spherical, small, surface smooth.

Skeleton spicules nearly straight, cylindrical, slender, rather abruptly pointed, entirely microspined; spines few, low, conical.

Dermal spicules absent or undetermined. (A few minute forms sometimes slightly curved, cylindrical but inflated near the middle, may be only the initial condition of the birotulates before their disks have been fully developed.)

Birotulates surrounding the gemmules very numerous and symmetrical, their outer rotulæ forming a smooth exterior to the gemmule. Shafts nearly cylindrical, but rapidly widening immediately under the rotules; frequently with a single spine near the middle. Umbonate rotulæ large, flat; margins finely laciniulate, often microspined upon both surfaces.

Meas. Skeleton spicules 0·0107 by 0·0005 inches. Birotulates 0·0012 by 0·00015 inches. Diameter of rotules 0·00075 inches.

Loc. Collected from Sherwood Lake near DeLand, Florida, by Henry Mills, Esq.

Respectfully dedicated to my friend Mr. Mills of Buffalo N. Y. to whose perseverence as a collector we owe this and the following beautiful species; the first new forms from the state of Florida; besides specimens of *S. fragilis*, *M. fluviatilis* and *H. ryderi* at this southernmost point of their range.

(10) **Meyenia subdivisa**, Potts. (Pl. IX, fig. vi.)

Sponge green when growing in the light, massive, encrusting; texture compact; composed of thick lines of fasciculated spicules and having a peculiarly vitreous, glistening appearance when dried. Surface smooth or rising into more or less abrupt rounded prominences, *near* the extremities of which the efferent osteoles are found. Pores numerous, conspicuous.

Gemmules few, spherical, resembling in appearance those of the genus *Heteromeyenia*; granular crust very thick.

Skeleton spicules cylindrical, robust, abruptly pointed, smooth; the smaller ones more or less microspined. In many places at the surface they gather into flocculent or wool-like masses, compactly grouped, without interspaces. (See remarks on *Tubella pennsylvanica*.)

Dermal spicules absent or undiscovered.

Birotulate spicules surrounding the gemmules very numerous; so crowded that some become displaced and, standing out beyond the others, simulate the appearance of the longer class of birotulates in *Heteromeyenia*. As all are of the same general shape however, and nearly of the same size, it is thought best to retain the species in the present genus. These spicules are very robust and the abundance of silicious material is evidenced by the repeated subdivision of every ray and spine. (Pl. IX, fig. vi, e. e. e.) Shafts cylindrical, frequently spined; rotules flat, irregularly circular, notched but slightly at the margin. Short rays subdivided.

Meas. Skeleton spicules 0·01 by 0·0006 inches. Birotulate spicules 0·0017 by 0·0003 inches. Diameter of rotules 0·0009 inches.

Hab. On submerged timber etc.

Loc. Collected by Mr. H. Mills in St. John's River near Palatka, Florida.

Dr. Bowerbank has remarked (Proc. Zool. Soc. 1863, p. 443, etc.) upon the number and variety of sponge spicules noticed by him in a collection of infusorial earth, made by Prof. Bailey in Florida; and from this fact and the descriptions of other travellers it has long seemed to me an ideally favorable place for the growth of sponges.

As circumstances prevented personal exploration in that direction, repeated efforts have been made to enlist the assistance of intending visitors, in the search for them; and much disappointment was felt when one friend, a most successful collector in other lines of natural history, reported that he could find none, attributing his failure and their apparent absence to the abundance of confervæ covering every probable place of their growth.

Since these failures Mr. Mills has made two visits to Florida; both during the latter part of our winter season, say from February to April; and the experience gained in many Northern waters has helped him to success in these. He has gathered several familiar species of *Spongilla*, *Meyenia*, *Heteromeyenia*, and *Tubella*, beside the two novel forms just described. The first of these, *M. millsii*, approaches *M. fluviatilis*, but differs from any of its varieties in the character of its rotules, which, instead of being deeply cut into rays, are delicately fringed or laciuulated like those of the smaller class of birotulates in *H. ryderii*. (Compare Pl. X, fig. ii, with Pl. XI, fig. v. c. c. c.)

The finest specimen of *M. subdivisa* grew upon the bark of a submerged pine log in the St. John's River, near Palatka, and covered it to the extent of two or more square feet, by an average of one half or three fourths of an inch in thickness. Its peculiarities are perhaps sufficiently stated above, but I remember being much impressed by the vitreous appearance mentioned, as suggesting that of the tropical South American forms of *Tubella*, *Parmula* and *Uruguaya*. A further search at points nearer the Southern extremity of the peninsula may give us some of these.

(11) **Meyenia (Spongilla) baileyi**, Bk. Proc. Zool. Soc. etc. 1863, p. 451.

"Sponge coating; surface smooth? Oscula and pores inconspicuous. Dermal membrane spiculous; spicula fusiform-acerate, entirely spined: spines of the middle cylindrical, truncated, very long and large. Skeleton spicula subfusiform-acerate, rather slender. Interstitial membranes spiculous; spicula same as those of the dermal membrane. Ovaria globular, smooth, abundantly spiculous; spicula arranged in lines radiating from the centre to the circumference of the ovary; birotulate; rotulæ irregularly and deeply cleft at the margins, incurvate; shaft very long, cylindrical, entirely spined; spines conical. Color in the dried state dark green." Bowerbank.

"*Hab.* A stream on Canterbury Road, West Point, New York."

(See remarks as to *Heteromeyenia repens*.)

(12) **Meyenia (Spongilla) capewelli**, Bk. Proc. Zool. Soc. etc. 1863, p. 447.

"Sponge massive, sessile; surface uneven, often lobular, smooth. Oscula simple, minute, dispersed. Pores inconspicuous. Dermal membrane pellucid, aspiculous; skeleton spicula acerate, rather short and stout. Ovaria subglobose; spicula birotulate, rather long, disposed in lines radiating from the centre of the ovary; rotulæ flat, margins slightly and irregularly crenulate; shafts slender, incipiently spinous, varying in length from one to one and a half diameter of a rotula. Color dull green, with a tint of yellow." Bowerbank.

Hab. Lake Hindmarsh, Victoria, Australia."

(13) **Meyenia anonyma**, Carter. Ann. and Mag. etc. 1881, p. 95.

"Sponge unknown, statoblast flask shaped; aperture terminal; composed of a membranous coat, striated longitudinally, supporting a reticulation consisting of extremely minute, erect, conical processes with their sharp ends inwards, and presenting in the centre of each interstice, especially towards each fundus, a short, thick, somewhat hour-glass-shaped spicule, whose outer end is more or less denticulated and whose inner one is inserted into the striated coat. Investing membrane of the germinal matter transparent, presenting the usual polygonal reticulation without granules, like compressed cell-structure." Carter.

Loc. River Amazons.

(14) **Meyenia ramsayi**, W. A. Haswell. Proc. Linn. Soc. New South Wales, 1882, p. 209.

"Sponge massive, tubercular, with finger-like projections.

Skeleton-spicules curved, abruptly pointed, smooth.

Birotulate spicules, shafts cylindrical, with one to ten prominent spines; rotulæ deeply dentate; twelve to twenty teeth.

Loc. Bell River at Wellington, Australia." Haswell.

(15) **Meyenia crateriformis**, Potts. Proc. Acad. Nat. Sci. etc. 1882, p. 12. (Pl. V, fig. vi. Pl. X, fig. v.)

Sponge encrusting, thin; texture very loose, forming no tangible skeleton.

Gemmules small, white, very numerous, visible from the upper or outer side of the sponge. Granular crust relatively extraordinarily thick, embedding slender spicules of great length. The foraminal tubule, standing at the centre of a crater-like depression amongst these, has suggested the specific name. In position the shafts of these long birotulates are rarely parallel, but, leaning to each side, cross each other in a perplexing and beautiful manner. (Pl. V. fig. vi.)

Skeleton spicules slender, fusiform, gradually pointed, sparsely and minutely microspined.

Dermal spicules somewhat apocryphal. (While smooth, slender, cylindrical forms that seem to be such, prove, in their further development, to have been merely immature birotulates, pertaining to the gemmules, there *are* others, still more slender and acuminate, that *may* be strictly dermal.)

Birotulates of the gemmules very long and slender; shaft cylindrical, whose length is five or six times the diameter of the supported rotules; abundantly spined, more particularly near the ends; spines long, cylindrical, rounded or recurved. Rotules composed of 3 to 6 short, recurved hooks with finely acuminate points. (Pl. X, fig. v, b,b,b,).

Meas. Diameter of gemmules 0·013 inches. Skeleton spicules 0·01 by 0·0004 inches. Length of birotulate spicules 0·0025 inches. Diameter of rotules 0·0004 ; of shaft 0·00015 inches.

Hab. On fixed or floating timber in shallow water.

Loc. Crowe's Mill, Brandywine Creek; Ivy Mills, Chester Creek; Fairmount Dam, Schuylkill River; and League Island and Lambertville, Delaware River, Pennsylvania.

The tradition that associates the Brandywine Battle Ground with the vision Lord Percy is said to have had of such a scene before leaving England, as the spot where he should meet his death in battle, is so far justified by the fact that it is indeed one of the loveliest scenes in Pennsylvania. These undulating hills, crowned with forest or waving with golden grain; the emerald meadows lining the broad stream on either side; the smaller brooklets gathering in the hollows and gurgling among the rocks, as they wind their way down to the main stream, form a scene of peace and tranquility which it is difficult to fill, in our own imaginations, with conflict and bloodshed or cover with the "thunder clouds of war."

It lay thus peacefully one summer day in 1881, when our wagons drew up near the old fashioned grist and saw mills, then occupied by Mr. Frank Crowe, about one mile above Chadd's Ford, made famous on that Revolutionary occasion. Some of the party went "a-fishing," but of course sponge hunting was the order of the day with the writer. Drawing on high rubber boots, I waded into the stream where the broad mill-race, a creek in itself though but a small portion of the Brandywine, narrows into the forebay and hurries on to the clattering wheels. At this point a rock-built overflow, like a dam breast, had checked a number of nearly water-logged timbers, and others were aground in the shallow water below. Many of these when turned over disclosed specimens of a filmy gray sponge, branching off here and there along the surface of the wood, yet with a curious want of continuity, as if its particles, in their haste to march forward, had neglected to keep open communication with their base of supplies. All along the lines and dotting the broader portions, small white or yellowish gemmules gleamed through the thin dermis, instead of being buried as in most other sponges in the deeper parts of the tissues.

This was the first discovery of *M. crateriformis*; it was afterward found in somewhat similar situations and with like characteristics in several other Pennsylvanian streams. So far as I remember, none of this species has reached me from abroad, except in one instance, where the situation and circumstances were entirely dissimilar. They will be found described in association with the sketch of *Meyenia plumosa*.

M. crateriformis was far from being the only sponge found on the occasion above described. In the lower corner of each mill, where the water boiled and rushed as it escaped from under the wheels, the stones and timbers bore many specimens of *S. lacustris*, *S. fragilis* and *M. fluviatilis*, The growth of the second of these, upon timbers lining the inner walls of the grist mill, was particularly abundant, nearly white and full of segregated spores.

(16) **Meyenia everetti**, Mills. Proc. Am. Soc. Micros. 1884. (Pl. X, fig. iii, and iv.)

Sponge green, without sessile portion, but consisting altogether of slender meandering filaments, little more than a sixteenth of an inch in diameter; made up of central lines of closely fasciculated skeleton spicules, with short thin lines of the same, diverging at angles of 30 to 50 degrees, and, on the surface, numerous single spicules, as yet unplaced, and forming no proper network. Near their ends the fronds were abruptly reduced, nearly to the diameter of the central band of spicules, and appeared to terminate in a sharp point.

Gemmules few but unusually large, as the crust is thick and the embedded birotulates are longer than in most other species. They are found axially, in a single series, along the fronds; each enclosed in a rather loosely formed capsule or cage of skeleton spicules, the diameter of which is much greater than that of the included gemmule.

Skeleton spicules slender, cylindrical, gradually or more abruptly pointed, smooth. (Pl. X, fig. iii and iv, a.a.a.)

Dermal spicules, minute *birotulates* with slender, cylindrical shafts, and cap-like rotules, notched at margin into five or six hooks. (Pl, X, as above, c.d.c.)

Birotulates surrounding the gemmules long, but variable in length. Shafts smooth, slender, particularly near the middle; widening and becoming almost club-shaped at the extremities, where the rotules are formed of five or six stout, recurved, acuminate hooks.

Meas. Diameter of gemmules 0·027 inches. Skeleton spicules 0·0082 by 0·0002 inches. Gemmule birotulates 0·0025 by 0·0001 inches. Diameter of rotule 0·0008 inches. Length of minute dermal birotulate 0·00063 inches.

Hab. On submerged grass, weeds etc. in shallow water.

Loc. Gilder Pond, Mt. Everett, Berkshire Co. Mass; collected by F. Wolle and H. S. Kitchel: MacKay's Lake, Pictou Co. Nova Scotia; Collected by A. H. MacKay.

My friends Dr. Francis Wolle and H. S. Kitchel Esq. of Bethlehem, Pennsylvania, in the pursuit of their favorite study of desmids and diatoms visited Mt. Everett near the extreme S.W. corner of Massachussetts, in September 1882. While devoted to their own specialty they yet in the spirit of true naturalists found real pleasure in gathering subjects in other departments of natural history, for the benefit of their absent friends.

In a note transmitting specimens and written immediately after their return, Mr. Kitchel says.—"Gilder Pond is a small pond some 1800 ft. above the sea, on the side of the mountain, fed by springs at the bottom and the drainage from still higher ground; no inlet, and no outlet except a small stream, which drains through the ground at one end." "It is almost entirely surrounded by rocks and the water is very pure and cold." "The sponge was first found upon the ground in shallow water; afterward in great quantities on submerged bushes etc. along the edge of the pond."

A card from Dr. Wolle a few days later gave the elevation as 2400 feet. The rough sketches prepared by both gentlemen to suggest its appearance while growing, indicated a delicate branching sponge, but the specimens sent had been packed between cards and forwarded by letter; in one case, at least, after partial decomposition in a bottle of water. There was nothing therefore in the fragments themselves to convince me of their external form except the suggestive presence of the broad bands of fasciculate skeleton spicules referred to in the description.

Four years passed before I was able, by my own observations, to verify the impression so vaguely gathered. It was during the last week of September 1886 that I journeyed for the first time, to Gilder Pond, with the primary object of determining the character of this sponge. Primary but not sole, for no one familiar with the beauty of the Berkshire Hills, would quite credit the assertion that even the most enthusiastic naturalist could limit his enjoyment of them to the act of gathering an insignificant sponge from a tarn upon the mountain side.

No, I saw and enjoyed all that the summer tourist enjoys, the sombre forests, the lichen-covered rocks; the mountain summits near at hand, the wide extended view which each gave to its visitors. I also climbed Mt. Everett, "the dome of the Taconics," and sat alone, the center of an unbroken horizon, embracing hundreds of square miles of such varied beauty as may well be the memory of a life time;—but to all this was added the unspeakable charm of a morning spent on the bosom of that little lake, shut in by the silent woods, its flora and its fauna clearly revealed through the bright waters below me. I will not believe that a scientific interest in natural objects can lessen one's enjoyment of the sights and the sounds, the scents and the colors that greet him; the reviving touch of the evening breeze or the exhilarant purity of this mountain air; it adds, instead, a sixth sense, the hope or the joy of discovery.

I found the present species very abundant and others hardly less so; one of them I shall have occasion to describe hereafter. *M. everetti* was widely spread over the bottom of the pond, not on the mud however, the sedimentary alluvium that had gathered here to a great depth; but on the water-weeds and grasses, the submerged verdure, over which it had crawled in slender threads, reaching from leaf to stem and from blade to leaf, as if some giant spider had spun them; but even more like the wavering, inconsequent trail left by a snail or an earth-worm to mark its nightly wanderings. With arm bared and fingers used as a rake, I could gather it plentifully; but its lines were so utterly flaccid that they at once became matted and massed together so as to lose all individuality. Some, now in the bottle at my side, were immersed almost immediately in alcohol, which hardened and preserved it.

This species is a very interesting one, furnishing the first instance among fresh-water sponges, in which the dermal spicule, generally a slender, smooth or more or less spiniferous acerate, is here seen as a well defined and symmetrical *birotulate*. Mr. Carter has kindly brought to my notice a very similar spicule occupying a like position in the marine form *Halichondria birotulata*, Higgins, from the West Indies and S. Australia; but in the case of those from fresh-waters, we have had nothing more definite than the immature or apocryphal forms in *M. crateriformis*. The very peculiar dermal spicules characterizing *M. plumosa* are most suggestive of this, or possibly, of a still more advanced type. (*Spongilla böhmii* and *S. novæ terræ*, were discovered later.)

The re-discovery of this species among the magnificent collections of sponges made by Mr. MacKay from the water-shed and other lakes abounding in Pictou County, Nova Scotia, gave me great pleasure, as showing the persistence of the type in widely separated districts; and for the confirmation it afforded of my previous observation, as to the general strengthening of spicular features in sponges as their localities approach sea-level.

(17) **Meyenia plumosa,** Carter; (*Spongilla plumosa,* Carter.) Ann. and Mag. Nat. Hist. 1849, p. 81.

"Massive, lobate. Structure feathery, fibrous, friable. Color greenish or light-brown. Skeleton-spicule curved, fusiform, gradually sharp-pointed, smooth. Flesh-spicule stelliform, consisting of a variable number of arms of various lengths radiating from a large, smooth globular body; arms spined throughout; spines longest at the ends, so as to present a capitate appearance, and recurved generally; the whole varying from a simple, spinous linear spicule to the stellate form first mentioned, thus modified by the size and presence of the globular inflation and number of arms developed from the centre of the former; abundant in all parts of the structure, but especially in the neighborhood of the statoblasts. Statoblast ellipsoidal; aperture lateral, infundibular; crust, which is thick and composed of granular microcell-substance, charged with birotulate spicules consisting of a long, straight, sparsely spiniferous shaft whose spines are large, conical and perpendicular, terminated at each end by an umbonate disk of equal size, whose margin is irregularly denticulated, with the processes more or less turned inwards, arranged perpendicularly, with one disk resting on the chitinous coat and the other forming part of the surface of the crust." Carter.

Loc. Bombay.

Meyenia plumosa, var. **palmeri**, Potts. Proc. U. S. Natl. Museum, 1885, p. 587. (Pl. X, fig. vi.)

Sponge (as seen in a dry state) dark brown, massive, attached to and surrounding the dependent branches of small trees whose stems are flooded by the spring freshets. Texture very loose and when dry so brittle that the dermal surface cannot be satisfactorily examined. (The impression conveyed by the interior appearance of this sponge is that it is made up of an infinite number of radiating, confluent branches.)

Gemmulæ large, numerous throughout the deeper portions of the sponge; subspherical or ovoid, surrounded by long birotulates imbedded in a granular crust.

Skeleton spicules straight or slightly curved, mainly cylindrical but gradually sharp-pointed, sparsely microspined. (Pl. X. fig. vi, a.)

Dermal spicules irregularly stellate as in the typical species, but, in the specimens examined, much fewer in number. They vary from simple acerates with one or more long divergent branches to beautiful radiate-spherical bodies whose rays are nearly equal, spined, and capitate by reason of recurved spines at their extremities. (ibid. e, e, c, f.) Another form of spicule, probably also dermal, of which several are seen upon nearly every slide prepared for microscopic examination, is very difficult of description. It may be said to be composed of an irregular series of smooth, curved rays arising from a nearly common centre, and is somewhat suggestive of a hedgehog or Scotch terrier. (ibid, g. g.)

Birotulate spicules pertaining to the gemmulæ, in length about three times the diameter of the supported rotules; shafts cylindrical, plentifully spined; spines long, conical. Outer surface of rotules convex, margins lacinulate; ends of incomplete rays obtuse, recurved. (ibid. b, c, d.)

Sponge masses subspherical, reaching five or six inches in diameter.

This sponge, collected by Dr. Edward Palmer along the banks of the Colorado River, near Lerdo, Sonora, in Northwestern Mexico, about 59 miles S.S.W. from Fort Yuma, California, is a valuable addition to the sponge fauna of this continent and interesting from the fact that the typical species, *M. plumosa* of Carter, has hereto-

fore only been found in his original locality, the rock water-tanks of
Bombay, East Indies. That it should skip a whole hemisphere and
only be found the second time at its own antipodes is indeed remarkable.

The lower reaches of the Colorado of the West extend for miles
through a region described by the collector as "the hottest, driest,
and most barren in the United States," whose "vegetation consists of
mesquit, cacti, and the screw-bean, *Strombocarpus pubescens.*" Its
normal border lands are known as the "first" and "second bottoms," of which the latter are the higher and of course more distant
from the channel. By the frequent changes in its bed however,
the river cuts through these and, washing away the one and filling
up the other, reverses their physical conditions. Upon the "second
bottoms" then, said to be only reached to any considerable depth
by the annual floods occurring during parts of May and June,
and not to continue flooded more than six weeks at a time, the
screw-bean abounds. It is described as a small tree of the general
appearance of a peach tree, but with more slender, drooping branches.
More or less of an alkaline deposit whitens the ground upon which
they grow, and the approaching traveler is puzzled to see in strong
contrast with it, hundreds or even thousands of dark masses, "like
wasp's nests," suspended two or three feet above.

It was this conundrum that confronted Dr. Palmer during his
recent visit, and the answer we have in the sponge before us. From
the Amazon River in the tropics to the waters of Maine and Nova
Scotia in the temperate regions of the north, sponges have long been
known to affect the pendent branches of stream-bordering bushes;
but it is unlikely that they have ever before been observed in such
quantities suspended for nine or ten months of the year over land
parched and desolate.

On referring to the earlier descriptions of his discoveries, by H. J.
Carter, we find that though he collected this species on two or
more occasions, the fragments were always found detached from
their place of growth and floating upon the surface in the
water-tanks referred to, about one month after the rainy season
had commenced. He believed that the vitality of the gemmules
was preserved during the dry season, notwithstanding their exposure to the sun and desiccating winds, and that their germination
after the water had again reached them was followed by a very rapid
growth of new sponge. This would seem to have been the case also

with the present variety as, according to the reports of the collector, the masses could not have been submerged for a greater period than six weeks in any one year. Whether the whole bulk as now seen was attained during a single season, or is the cumulative result of several annual growths of the persistent masses, cannot now be determined. (See description of *Parmula brownii*.)

It is worthy of notice that *M. plumosa* and this variety, v. *palmeri;* differ from all other known fresh-water sponges by the presence in them of a compound or substellate dermal spicule. The spiculæ of the dermis throughout the group are generally minute, spined accrates; in *M. everetti*, Mills, we find them as minute birotulates. In *this* species the two forms seem to be combined; the spines have become central and prolonged, while their capitate extremities suggest the rotules of the last-named species.

Of the six sponge masses from the above locality, sent by the Smithsonian Institution for examination, the smallest was somewhat fusiform in shape and proved to belong to a different species, *Meyenia crateriformis*, Potts, heretofore found along the eastern border of the United States. In it alone, the mass was not darkened by the presence of some pervading vegetable parasite.

(III) Gen. HETEROMEYENIA, Potts.

Proc. Acad. Nat. Sci. Phil., 1881, p. 150. (Pl. VI, fig. i.)

Gen. char. Skeleton spicules and gemmulæ as in *Meyenia;* the latter surrounded by intermingled birotulates of *two classes*, generally differing in form, and whose shafts are of unequal lengths. The proximal disks of all rest upon the chitinous coat; the outer extremities of the less numerous class projecting beyond the others.

This genus now covers at least three well defined species, with several marked varieties, and represents a type or modification of *Meyenia* unknown to Mr. Carter at the time of the preparation of his system. It was founded in 1881 upon the discovery of *H. repens* and *H. argyrosperma* at Lehigh Gap, Pennsylvania; and its necessity was confirmed shortly after by the addition of *H. ryderi*, and its several varieties. It will be seen by the genus definition that it is not intended to embrace mere irregularities in the positions or in the length of gemmule-birotulates, such as may sometimes be found in *M. everetti* or *M. subdivisa;* nor yet to include biserial or triserial arrangements of them. In each of the three principal species described there are essential differences, not merely in the length but in the forms of these birotulates; those of the longer class in each case being terminated by long, hooked rays, while the rotules of the others are larger, flatter and more delicately divided. (Pl. XI.)

KEY TO THE SPECIES OF THE GENUS HETEROMEYENIA.

1. Rays of long birotulates noticeably incurved like fish-hooks; rotulæ of shorter class mushroom shaped; shafts generally smooth. Dermal spicules present. (Pl. XI, fig. iii.)
H. repens.
2. Rays of long birotulates few, (1 to 4) long, stout and claw-like; shafts with few spines; rotulæ of smaller class very irregular; shafts abundantly spined. (Pl. XI, fig. i and ii.)
H. argyrosperma.
3. Rotulæ of long birotulates small; rays hooked; shafts spiniferous: rotulæ of smaller class large, flat; margins lacinulate or delicately rayed; shafts generally smooth. (Pl. XI, fig. iv, v, and vi.)
H. ryderi.

(1) **Heteromeyenia repens,** Potts. Proc. Acad. Nat. Sci. Phila. 1881, p. 150. (Pl. XI, fig. iii.)

Spongilla repens, Potts. Proc. etc., 1880, p. 357.

Sponge bright green, encrusting, thin. Texture loose and incoherent; the projecting lines of skeleton spicules giving it a peculiarly rough appearance.

Gemmulæ not very abundant, spherical; with granular crust imbedding two classes of birotulate spicules as described.

Skeleton spicules rather slender, subfusiform, sparsely microspined; gradually pointed.

Dermal spicules fusiform, nearly straight, entirely spined; spines cylindrical, rounded; those near the middle perpendicular, much longer than the others.

Gemmule-birotulates of the longer class comparatively few, standing amongst the others; shafts smooth or microspined, nearly cylindrical, often irregularly bent. Rotulæ dome-shaped, the ends of the recurved rays still further incurved like fish-hooks; terminations rounded. (Pl. XI, fig. iii, b.b.)

Birotulates of the shorter class very numerous and symmetrical, about ⅔ the length of the others; shafts generally largest near the middle, or least near the rotules; often with one or more conspicuous spines. Curvature of the rotules like that of a mushroom, or rather flat umbrella; rays not deeply notched; rounded or slightly incurved. (Pl. XI, fig. iii, c.c.c.)

Meas. Skeleton spicules 0·0111 by 0·00045 inches. Dermal spicules 0·0025 by 0·0001 inches. Shaft of long birotulates 0·0029 by 0·00015 inches; diameter of rotule 0·0009 inches. Length of short birotulates 0·00168 inches; diameter of its rotules 0·0007 inches.

Hab. On plants, timber, etc., in shallow water.

Loc. In the pool at Lehigh Gap, Pennsylvania; in Lake Hopatcong, New Jersey, and at other places along the Eastern coast of the United States.

Lehigh Gap, frequently mentioned as a locality in these descriptions, is a rail-road station and quiet watering place, where the Lehigh River forces its way through the Blue Mts. in Carbon County, Pennsylvania. The mountain chain or ridge, with an elevation of about eleven hundred feet above the river, is here abruptly cut through by it, leaving on one side precipitous, jagged edges of bare rock; while on the other it more gradually slopes from the river to the summit.

Nearly at the narrowest point the river is crossed by an old time suspension bridge depending from chains composed of long iron links. On the bank of the river just below, there stands, or until quite recently stood, the ruin of an old mill, that had been burned before the memory of the oldest inhabitant. The mill race, passing under an archway through its walls, was choked by the fallen and blackened timbers, amongst which the water could hardly have been said even to creep, excepting when a freshet in the adjacent river supplied its fauna and flora with a momentary draught of fresh water.

It so chanced that during the early days of my enthusiasm for sponge collecting, curiosity led me to look into this pool, in reality little more than a very wet cellar, with the result of adding a new genus (*Heteromeyenia*) to the system of fresh water sponges, with two species pertaining to the same; also a variety of *Spongilla fragilis*, a form of *Meyenia fluviatilis* and a new species (*T. pennsylvanica*) of the genus *Tubella*, its first discovery in other waters than those of the River Amazons, South America. Numerous specimens of the higher types of minute aquatic life; fine species of *Bryozoa* etc., gave added interest to this field of work.

On October 13th., 1880 the first specimen of *H. repens* was discovered upon the stems and leaves of a *Potamogeton*, by my friend and companion Mr. J. S. Cheyney; and after reaching home I found that I had, myself, collected others from the fallen timbers, without recognizing their novelty. Its habit was to creep over submerged timbers and sticks, the leaves of water plants, the slender stems of *Nitella* etc., generally, when upon a smooth surface, assuming vermiform lines, one fourth inch or more in width, along which the gemmules were left in scattered groups. Five years later I found it growing in a similar fashion in Lake Hopatcong, New Jersey.

I have been thus particular to give the history of this species because of the doubt that may disturb other minds than my own, whether it may not be identical with *Meyenia (Spongilla) baileyi*, of Bowerbank; the sponge that Prof. Bailey gathered "from a stream on the Canterbury Road, near West Point, New York." Admitting the resemblance of the spicules that Dr. B. has represented and described, to some of those pertaining to this species, I would call attention to the fact that he has neither described nor represented the more numerous class of birotulate spicules, which, under the supposition that the species were identical, would be a singular omission. If stress be laid upon the resemblance of the dermal spicules of the two forms, I remark that two species of *Carterius* (*C. tubisperma* and *C. latitenta*) have a similar one. The type specimen from which the description by Dr. B. was prepared, was a very small one and I have not had access to it for final comparison. For these reasons and while a doubt remains as to their identity, I incline to hold fast by my descriptive title.

(2) **Heteromeyenia argyrosperma**, Potts. Proc. Acad. Nat. Sci. Phila. 1881, p. 150. (Pl. VI. fig. i.)

Spongilla argyrosperma, Potts. (Proc. Acad. etc., 1880, p. 357.) Sponge minute, encrusting; color gray; texture loose.

Gemmulæ abundant; relatively large, on account of the unusually thick granular crust, through which the distal ends of the longer class of surrounding birotulates sometimes project, or support portions of it in many conical prominences. (Pl. VI, fig. i.) Foraminal tubule somewhat prolonged; smallest at the extremity. Color silvery white, suggesting the specific name.[1]

Skeleton spicules rather slender, cylindrical or sub-fusiform; abruptly pointed, sparsely spiniferous; spines small, pointed; projecting forward towards the extremities of the spicules. (Pl. XI, fig. i, a.a.)

---

[1] If this and some other of the specific names, derived from the Greek, are found not to be in "good form," I can only regret that the discovery of the rule came too late, and that *many alterations* of name may be a worse error.

Dermal spicules apparently wanting.

Gemmule birotulates of the larger class very robust; shafts long, irregularly cylindrical, often bent, occasionally spinous; spines long, pointed, perpendicular or recurved. Rays of the rotulæ one to four, assuming the form of strong, claw-like hooks, recurved and incurved. (Pl. XI, fig. i, b.b.)

Shorter birotulates much smaller, abundantly spined; spines long, conical. Rotules flatter, irregularly hooked. (Pl. XI, fig. i, c.c.c.)

Meas. Skeleton spicules 0·0109 by 0·0004 inches. Long birotulates 0·00543 by 0·0003 inches. Diameter of disks or hooks 0·0012 inches. Length of short birotulates 0·0028 inches. Diameter of disk 0·0007 inches.

Hab. On submerged sticks, stones, etc.

Loc. Lehigh Gap and Holicong, Pennsylvania; New England States, New Jersey, Nova Scotia, etc.

No other sponge as yet found in American waters, can compare with this, in the robustness and positive characters of its birotulate spicules. It was first found at Lehigh Gap and has since been gathered and received from a few other places.

Notwithstanding its strong points, the sponge itself has been known to occur only as a delicate incrustation; or its whilom presence has been recognized by the discovery of the gemmules that had been left after nearly all its skeleton spicules had been washed away.

Heteromeyenia argyrosperma, var. **tenuis,** Potts. (Pl. XI, fig. ii.)

This variety of *H. argyrosperma* differs from the typical species chiefly in the extreme slenderness of all its parts.

Meas. Skeleton spicules 0·0087 by 0·0002 inches. Long birotulates 0·00438 by 0·00015 inches. Diameter of rotules or hooks 0·0006 inches. Length of short birotulate 0·00297 inches. Diameter of its rotules 0·0005 inches.

Loc. Harvey's Lake near Wilkes-Barre, Pennsylvania, and Lake Hopatcong, New Jersey.[1]

---

[1] It will be noticed that the slender forms of well known sponges which have, in this work, been uniformily designated as varieties, have been generally collected in waters at high altitudes, *S. lacustris,* v. *montana* at 2500 feet, (Pl. VIII, fig. vi); *S, fragilis,* v. *minuta,* 600 ft.; v. *minutissima* (Pl· VIII, fig. ii.) and v. *irregularis* 1200 feet; *H. argyrosperma,* v. *tenuis,* 1200 ft , (Pl. XI, fig. ii); and *Tuebila pennsylvanica,* v. *minima,* at 1800 feet above sea level. On the other hand *H. ryderi,*

Harvey's Lake, Pennsylvania, and Lake Hopatcong in Northern New Jersey, in nearly the same latitude, and with a common altitude of about 1200 feet, may be classed as mountain lakes, lying in the gorges between high hills, wooded or cultivated, and with no outlook in any direction. Of latter years, both have been enlarged and increased in depth by the construction of gates at their outlets. By this means the water has been raised and controlled, in the former, for milling purposes; in the latter, to use it as a feeder to the Morris Canal. In Lake Hopatcong the water thus "backed up" has found its way through cross-gorges into parallel valleys, originally heavily wooded, and the denuded stems and shorter stumps, standing up through the glittering water or resting in the shallows, suggest a prosaic if not a classical appropriateness, in the local name of one of them,—the "River Styx."

In this locality and in the so-called "Cedar Swamp," another deep bay in this nine-mile-long pond, I found my principal sport as a collector. The season (the last of October,) was perhaps rather late for the species represented; but on nearly every floating log or fallen tree top, or loosened stump, could be found when they were turned over, shining patches of white or yellowish gemmules, left in groups upon the smooth surface or partly hidden in little crevices of bark or root. No conspicuous sponge masses, few even of the filmy layers of skeleton spicules; only these scattering and loosely placed aggregations. Great numbers of them were chipped off and dried for more particular examination in the laboratory.

This kind of collecting has been found far more productive of interesting species than where one limits himself to the larger, green sponges. Though not a single massive sponge had been discovered, representatives were collected of three forms of *S. fragilis*, two of *H. argyrosperma*, one of *H. repens*, besides many specimens of *Tubella pennsylvanica*.

---

v. *baleni*, (Pl. XI, fig. iv.) came from near Plainfield, New Jersey and from Florida, in both, presumably, at a low level; and one of the most robust forms of *S. lacustris* seen in this country, was gathered from an "Ice Lake" in the Sierra Nevada Mts. at an altitude of 7000 feet. (Pl. VII, fig. i.)

If a reason be sought to account for the prevailing rule in these cases, the plausible suggestion may of course be made, that the water of lakes upon dividing ridges or high table-lands may be deficient in the silicious constituent that would be acquired later, from violent contact with rocks in the bed of mountain streams, etc.; but a much longer series of observations and exact chemical analysis will be needed to make this observation any more than a guess.

(4) **Heteromeyenia longistylis**, Mills. Proc. Am. Soc. of Microscopists 1884 p. 16.

Sponge unknown.

Gemmulæ large, spherical; crust thick.

Skeleton spicules slender, cylindrical to sub-fusiform; gradually pointed, very sparsely microspined.

Dermal spicules fusiform, entirely spined; spines near the middle long, cylindrical; terminations rounded.

Shafts of the larger class of birotulates relatively very long, cylindrical, often bent, generally smooth. Hooks of rotulæ recurved and incurved.

Rotules of the shorter class of birotulates flatter; shafts cylindrical, spinous; spines short, conical.

Meas. Skeleton spicules 0·0103 by 0·00025 inches. Length of dermal spicules 0·0023 inches. Long birotulates 0·0049 by 0·00015 inches. Diameter of disk 0·0009 inches. Length of short birotulate 0·0032 inches. Diameter of its disk 0·0008 inches.

Loc. Lehigh River, Bethlehem, Pa.(?) Collected by Dr. Wolle.

I had been inclined to consider the above merely a variety of *H. argyrosperma*, but the mention of dermal spicules in my description, prepared several years ago from a very minute fragment, has induced me to give it the benefit of the doubt, until the sponge itself can be again collected.

(3) **Heteromeyenia ryderi**, Potts. Proc. Acad. Nat. Sci. Phila. 1882, p. 13. (Pl. XI, fig. iv, v and vi.)

Sponge light green, massive, often hemispherical; texture loose; surface more or less lobed.

Gemmulæ numerous, spherical, relatively smaller than in *H. argyrosperma*; crust thick; foramina inconspicuous, short, tubular.

Skeleton spicules non-fasciculate, fusiform, gradually pointed, entirely spined, except at the extremities; spines broadly conical, often projected forward, towards the terminations of the spicules. (Pl. XI, figs. iv to vi, a,a, etc.)

Dermal spicules wanting.

Long birotulates variable in relative numbers, shafts cylindrical, spined; spines equal in length with the rays of the rotulæ; hooked or curved from the extremities; rotulæ of three to six short, recurved hooks; sometimes umbonate or with a spinous termination. (Ibid. b,b, etc.)

Short birotulates with cylindrical shafts rapidly enlarging under the rotules, bearing one or more perpendicular spines. Diameter of rotules nearly as great as the length of the shaft; margins lacinulate or crenulate, outer surfaces flat, symmetrical, often microspined; terminations rounded. (Pl. XI, fig. v, c,d, etc.)

Meas. Skeleton spicules 0·0127 by 0·0006 inches. Long birotulates 0·0023 by 0·00025 inches. Diameter of disk 0·0006 inches. Length of short birotulates 0·0012 inches; diameter of its disk 0·0009 inches.

Hab. Timbers, stones, etc., in shallow flowing water.

Loc. Found from Florida to Nova Scotia, and from the Atlantic coast to Iowa, United States.

H. ryderi alone, of this genus, has been found large enough to attract the attention of a casual observer; inclining to form upon plane surfaces, hemispherical or dome-shaped masses several inches in diameter. In these and other cases they are made up of a congeries of lobes or rounded prominences. It was first found in the year 1881, rather plentifully, within a limited space upon the rocky bottom of Indian Run, a very small stream in the neighborhood of Philadelphia, Pennsylvania. The following year it was missing, and I have never since found it in that stream. It has been gathered or received from at least nine American States mostly along the Atlantic coast from Nova Scotia to Florida, but including one remittance from the western state of Iowa. The finest specimen collected was from the timber side of the fore-bay of E. Doughty's mill, Absecum, New Jersey. This was about three inches in diameter and more than two inches in thickness.[1]

H. ryderi has furnished me with my latest and most valuable lesson in group classification. Until quite recently the species stood compact, or with only the single suggested variety, *H. baleni*, where the spicular features were similar, though more slender, and the general form of the sponge had not been particularly observed.

---

[1] The circumstance above mentioned as to the failure to find this species at the same place during successive seasons, is a peculiarity of habit only too familiar to sponge collectors. However reliable their recurrence may be in *lakes* or *ponds*, in our smaller *streams* the fact that a species was found at a given locality during one season, furnishes no guarantee for its reappearance there during the next. When *any* sponge is found, the probabilities are rather in favor of its belonging to a *different* species. In the present case, a year or two later, I found, a few yards further down the stream, not *H. ryderi* but *Tubella pennsylvanica*. From my favorite locality for *Carterius latitenta*, a friend, who undertook to bring me a fresh specimen, two or three years after its first discovery, sent me a fine form of *S. lacustris;* and so they go, constantly moving down stream; one species succeeding another as they travel on to the great sea and there—

Last autumn I collected in Gilder Pond, Berkshire Co. Massachusetts, already described, a sponge as different in its general appearance from the typical form of *H. ryderi*, as can well be imagined, but with similar birotulate spicules; and their very dissimilarity in external form led me to think of *H. pictovensis*, in which the gemmule spicules are also like those of *H. ryderi*. It was not at all willingly, but rather in spite of an exceedingly rebellious disinclination, that I came at last to the conclusion that the others had no sufficient claim to specific distinction, as *H. ryderi* typified and included them all.

The strongest member of this species is the variety *H. pictovensis*, next to be described. (Pl. XI, fig. vi.) I have only seen rather minute specimens of it, but believe it to be both massive and compact, and nearly smooth in surface and outline. A form found in the Lehigh River at White Haven, comes next, also with strongly spinous skeleton spicules and very robust birotulates. Then comes the typical form from Philadelphia, described above as externally hemispherical, but composed of compacted lobes. In the next v. *walshii*, from Gilder Pond, I imagine the lobes have separated and spread out into the slender, subdividing branches mentioned in the description of that variety. The series probably terminates with the delicate features of v. *baleni* (Pl. XI, fig. iv,) which will most likely be found also branching.

Heteromeyenia ryderi, v. pictovensis, Potts. Proc. Acad. Nat. Sci. Phila. 1885, p, 28. (Pl. XI, fig. vi.)

Sponge light green, even when dry; massive, encrusting. Texture very compact; spicules non-fasciculated, persistent. Surface mostly smooth.

Gemmules as discovered very scarce, spherical; crust thick.

Skeleton spicules cylindrical, short, robust, rounded or abruptly terminated, entirely spined; spines conical at the middle of the spicule, elsewhere generally curving forward toward each extremity. Rounded terminations of spicules covered with short spines, though frequently a single large spine or acute termination is seen at one or both ends. (Pl. XI, fig. vi, a,b,c.)

Dermal spicules absent or undiscovered.

Birotulates of the longer class surrounding the gemmules rather numerous, one third of their own length longer than the others; shafts mostly smooth, conspicuously fusiform, frequently with one or more long spines near the middle. Rotules consisting of three to six irregularly placed rays, recurved at their extremities. (Ibid. d,d,d.)

Birotulates of the shorter class abundant and compactly arranged around the gemmule; shafts mostly smooth, though sometimes bearing a single spine; irregularly cylindrical but rapidly thickening to support the rotules, which are large, umbonate, nearly flat, and finely lacinulate at their margins; occasionally microspined. (Ibid. e, e, e.)

Meas. Skeleton spicules 0·0075 by 0·00075 inches. Length of long birotulates 0·0021, of short birotulates 0·0012 inches. Diameter of disk of latter 0·0009 inches.

Hab. On submerged wood, etc.

Loc. Collected by A. H. MacKay Esq. of Pictou, Nova Scotia, from several lakes upon the water-shed of that region; and later, from similar situations in Newfoundland.

The close general agreement of the above description, (prepared while the writer was under the conviction that the sponge was a distinct species) with that just given of the typical *H. ryderi*, except as regards the robustness and spinous character of their skeleton spiculæ, (features that we have already seen to be extremely variable) will, I think, help to explain, perhaps to justify my present act in reducing it to the position of a variety of the latter. That there are obvious differences between them is unquestionable; that these differences are specific, I do not *now* believe.

This beautiful sponge was first discovered by Mr. A. H. MacKay during the summer of 1884, when its novelty, as indicated by its unusually robust, entirely spined skeleton spicules, was easily imagined; but the absence of gemmules at that time, precluded the determination of its generic relations, and it continued for a while unnamed. During the last week in December of the same year, a further search was rewarded by the finding of other "specimens upon sticks pulled up through a break made in the ice," and among these a few and but a few gemmules were discovered. These sufficed to place it clearly within the genus *Heteromeyenia*, with the final designation as indicated above.

The skeleton spicules of this variety are more entirely and conspicuously spined than those of any other known North American sponge. In some forms of *Meyenia fluviatilis* they are noticeably spiniferous, though the terminations are generally naked; in *Tubella pennsylvanica* they are entirely spined. The spicules of *Spongilla igloviformis* are marked with large, prickle-like spines; and amongst material collected at Deep Creek, Virginia, and also from sedimentary deposits in Nova Scotia, still another and more coarsely spined spicule has been collected, whose affiliations have not, as yet, been ascertained. *H.* v. *pictovensis* differs from all these in its *dense* spination and in the relatively great thickness and the rounded ends of its spicules.

Attention is asked for a moment to one fact stated by Mr. MacKay in his letter transmitting the last above specimens. They were gathered in midwinter from under the ice and were as I can testify, of a vivid green color and from *his* description were evidently still growing. The scarcity of gemmules may remind us of a similar condition in the case of *Spongilla aspinosa*, which has also been seen to be evergreen; and of the inference then suggested that they may not exist because they are not *needed*.

The form alluded to as having been found at White Haven has never been named, and does not need varietal designation. Its general spiculation is merely *more* robust than that of *H. ryderi* in a smaller degree than that in which the spicules of v. *baleni* seem *less* so. Intermediately must be placed,

Heteromeyenia ryderi, v. walshii, n. v.

Sponge light green; primarily sessile but soon sending out slender, subdividing branches, palmate, with rounded terminations; giving them a stag-horn-like appearance. Fronds made up of many slender, nearly parallel lines of slightly fasciculated spicules, the net work being completed by crossing lines of single or nearly solitary spicules.

Gemmules infrequent, spherical; crust rather slight.

Skeleton spicules slender, cylindrical, somewhat curved, gradually or more abruptly pointed, sparsely microspined.

Long birotulates with typical rotules of hooked rays; shafts inflated at the middle, with one to five long spines.

Rotules of short birotulates relatively large, flat; margins laciniulate; shafts smooth, thickening under the rotules.

Loc. Gilder Pond, Massachusetts.

During that solitary but most enjoyable morning spent upon Gilder Pond, as already described in my sketch of *M. everetti*, I discovered, early in my explorations, that there were beneath my boat *two* forms of branching sponges. They were not very dissimilar in size, that is, in the slenderness of their fronds; but in the one case these terminated abruptly in sharp points,—in the other they were rounded as above described, and reminded me of the broadly palmate antlers of a stag. On reaching my microscope their generic difference was quickly discovered.

The name I have attached to this variety is in acknowledgement of the exceptional courtesy shown and the assistance given me by Mr. T. L. Walsh, the owner of the pond and of the surrounding land upon the mountain side.

Heteromeyenia ryderi, v. baleni. (Pl. XI. fig. iv.)

Meas. Skeleton spicules 0·0072 by 0·00015 inches. Long birotulates 0·00185 by 0·000075 inches. Diameter of disk 0·0005 inches. Length of short birotulates 0·0012 inches. Diameter of its disk 0·0006 inches.

Loc. Plainfield, New Jersey; Florida etc.

This variety bears the same relation to its typical species that v. *tenuis* does to *H. argyrosperma*. All classes of spicules are very slender; but with this exception the associated forms resemble those of *H. ryderi*. It is dedicated to my friend Mr. A. D. Balen, who first collected it near Plainfield, New Jersey; but it has since been found in several localities, including the state of Florida where it was collected by Mr. Mills.

It has been remarked in my comments upon *Spongilla novæterræ* that intermediate forms connecting the genera distinguished by birotulate spiculæ, were frequent. One instance of this is found in the species before us. The genus *Heteromeyenia* is only distinguished from *Meyenia* by the presence of *two* dissimilar classes of birotulates. The numbers of those of the larger class are sometimes so reduced as to be with some difficulty detected; as in a form of *H. ryderi* sent me by Prof. Osborne from Ames, Iowa. In *Meyenia millsii*, from Florida, we have, what is essentially the same sponge, with this class entirely eliminated : as, however, there is left but one class, we can do no other than place that species among the *Meyeniæ*.

Since preparing the above, I have received two contributions of sponges from Mr. Fred. Mather, the intelligent and energetic superintendent of a hatching establishment at Cold Spring Harbor, Long Island, N. Y., under the care of the U. S. Fish Commission. Both of these have proved to be masses of *H. ryderi*. He reports them as growing plentifully throughout the winter, in their tanks and ponds, with the temperature frequently at 32° F. and below. The species therefore, in this region, as well as in Nova Scotia and New Foundland must be considered as at least occasionally perennial.

(IV.) Gen. TUBELLA, Carter.

Gen. char. Skeleton spiculæ as in the foregoing genera, but sometimes hemispherically rounded at the extremities. Gemmulæ globular or elliptical; apertures lateral or terminal. Granular crust charged with trumpet-shaped inæquibirotulate spicules, of which the larger rotule rests upon the chitinous coat; the size of the outer rotule smaller, but bearing a variable relation to that of the former. The margins of the larger rotules generally entire.

The genus *Tubella* was created by H. J. Carter in 1881 with four species, all from the River Amazon, in South America; one of them was of his own naming; the remaining three having been previously described (as Spongillas), by Dr. Bowerbank. The new genus was needed to separate those sponges having markedly unequal birotulates, from the typical forms of *Meyenia*. The discovery in Pennsylvania during the same year, of a fifth species and afterward of its wide distribution throughout the United States, tends to approve this necessity. Ann. and Mag. 1881, p. 96. (Pl. VI, fig. ii.)

KEY TO THE SPECIES OF THE GENUS TUBELLA.

1. Inæquibirotulate or trumpet-shaped spicules of two forms, upon separate gemmules. The shafts of one form stouter and bearing a larger distal rotule than that of the other. Flesh spicules wanting. *T. paulula.*
2. Shafts of trumpet-shaped spicules long, nearly cylindrical, spiniferous. Flesh spicules entirely spined. *T. spinata.*
3. Sponge structure rigid; terminations of skeleton spicules rounded. Gemmules surrounded by a capsule of spined spicules, much smaller than those of the skeleton. Shaft of trumpet-shaped spicules short, with a ring-like inflation near the larger rotule. *T. reticulata.*
4. Birotulates in two zones, *i. e.* trumpet-shaped next the chitinous coat, surrounded by a zone of short, robust spicules with equal rotules of eight recurved teeth or rays. *T. recurvata.*
5. Skeleton spicules spiniferous. No dermal spicules. Rotules of trumpet-shaped spicules flat or twisted; margins generally entire; shafts smooth. (Pl. VI, fig. ii.) *T. pennsylvanica.*

(1) **Tubella paulula,** Carter. Ann. and Mag. 1881, p. 96.

Spongilla paulula, Bowerbank. Proc. Zool. Soc. etc., 1863, p. 453.

Sponge "thin, encrusting. Surface even. Structure fragile, crumbling. Color now brown. Skeleton spicule curved, fusiform, abruptly sharp-pointed, spiniferous or smooth. Statoblast globular; aperture sunken, infundibular; crust composed of granular microcell structure, charged with two kinds of inæquibirotulates, one form of which is much stouter than the other, and consists of a straight shaft passing by trumpet-like expansion into the large disk, which often has radiating lines, and abruptly terminating in the other, which is only one fourth the diameter of the former; the other form similarly constucted, but more delicate, with the shaft inflated towards the large disk, and the smaller one much less in proportion than in the larger form; the forms not mixed but confined to their statoblasts respectively; arranged perpendicularly, with the large disk resting on the chitinous coat, and the smaller one forming part of the surface of the statoblast." Carter.

Loc. River Amazon.

(2) **Tubella spinata,** Carter. Ann. and Mag. 1881, p. 96.

Sponge "thin, coating, spreading. Structure fragile, crumbling. Color light brown. Skeleton spicule curved, fusiform, gradually sharp-pointed, smooth or spiniferous. Flesh spicule minute, curved, usiform, thin, gradually sharp-pointed, covered with perpendicular spines, which are longest about the centre. Statoblast elliptical, flask-shaped; aperture terminal; crust thick, composed of granular microcell-substance charged with inæquibirotulate spicules consisting of a straight shaft inflated near the small end, and passing by a trumpet-like expansion into the large disk. Sparsely spined; disk circular, smooth, with an even margin, small end consisting of a circular convex head, regularly denticulated on the margin with eight or more conical processes, which are slightly inclined towards the shaft; arranged perpendicularly, so that the disk rests on the chitinous coat and the head forms part of the surface of the statoblast." Carter.

Loc. River Amazon.

(3) **Tubella reticulata,** Carter. Ann. and Mag. 1881, p. 97.

Spongilla reticulata, Bowerbank. Proc. Zool. Soc. etc. 1863, p. 455.

Sponge "elliptical, or fusiform when growing round the immersed small branches of trees. Structure extremely rigid, reticulate, terminating in thorn-like processes on the surface. Color light sea-green when growing in clear water. Skeleton spicules curved or bent, cylindrical or subfusiform, rounded at the ends, absolutely smooth or sparsely spiniferous, becoming more so towards the statoblasts where they are not more than half the size, thickly spined, and in this shape form a distinct capsular layer around each of those organs. Statoblast elliptical, ovoid; aperture terminal; crust composed of granular microcell-substance, charged with inæquibirotulate spicules consisting of a straight shaft passing by trumpet-like expansion into the large disk, with two or more spines about the centre, and furnished with a ring-like inflation towards the disk; disk circular, smooth, with even margin, which is somewhat recurved, small end consisting of a circular umbonate head, regularly denticulated on the margin, with 6–8 conical processes, which are slightly inclined inwards or towards the shaft; arranged perpendicularly, so that the disk rests on the chitinous coat, and the head or small end forms part of the surface of the statoblast." Carter.

Loc. River Amazon.

(4) **Tubella recurvata,** Carter. Ann. and Mag. 1881, p. 98.

Spongilla recurvata, Bowerbank. Proc. Zool. Soc. etc. 1863, p. 456.

Sponge "sessile, coating. Surface even. Structure fragile, crumbling. Color brownish. Skeleton spicules curved, fusiform, abruptly sharp-pointed, smooth or spiniferous. Statoblast globular; aperture infundibular; crust thick, composed of granular microcell-substance charged with inæquibirotulate spicules, consisting of a delicate, straight, smooth shaft passing by trumpet-like expansion into the large disk, which is circular, smooth, saucer-shaped, inverted, with even margin, curved towards the shaft, and abruptly terminating in the other, which is only one eighth of the diameter of the disk, arranged perpendicularly with the large disk resting on the chitinous coat, and the small one somewhat within the surface of the crust; surrounded by a capsule of short thick spicules, consisting of a straight, smooth shaft, slightly inflated in the centre, and terminated at each end by an equal-sized head, which is prominently umbonate, with circular margin regularly divided into eight conical teeth slightly incurved, arranged perpendicularly around the statoblast, with one end free and the other adherent to the surface of the crust." Carter.

Loc. River Amazon; also Beni River, East Bolivia.

(5) **Tubella pennsylvanica,** Potts. Proc. Acad. Nat. Sci. Phila. 1882, p. 14. (Pl. VI, fig. ii, Pl. XII, figs. i, ii, iii.)

Sponge gray; or, when growing in the light, green; minute, incrusting; surface of mature specimens often found covered with parallel skeleton spicules, not yet arranged to form cell-like interspaces.

Gemmules very numerous, small; granular crust thin or thick; sometimes covering to a considerable depth, the outer extremities of the rotules, which in other cases project beyond it. (Pl. VI. fig. ii.)

Skeleton spicules extremely variable as to length and curvature; sub-fusiform, acuminate or rounded; entirely spined; spines large, conical; terminations mostly rounded. (Pl. XII, fig. i, ii and iii, a.a.a.)

Dermal spicules wanting.

Birotulate spicules surrounding the gemmules numerous, consisting of a large rotule next the chitinous coat; whilst the distal rotule varies in diameter from that of the connecting shaft to near equality with the other. Margin of large rotule generally entire; surface flat and table-like or irregularly exflected; smaller rotule obscurely angular or occasionally notched. Shafts widening toward the larger rotule, variable in length and thickness; always smooth. (ibid b. c. d. etc.)

Meas. Skeleton spicules 0·0066 by 0·0003 inches. Inæquibirotulates 0·00035 by 0·0001 inches. Diameter of large rotule 0.0007 inches; do, of smaller rotule 0·00015 inches.

Hab. On stones and timbers in shallow water.

Loc. Lehigh River and tributaries; also generally throughout the Eastern United States.

The first specimens of *T. pennsylvanica* were found in November 1881, among a miscellaneous collection of sponges from Lehigh Gap, where they had grown, at an altitude of about 600 ft. above sea level. They were minute, barely one fourth inch in diameter; but were welcomed with enthusiasm as the first representatives of the genus that had been discovered in North America or, in fact, anywhere except in the equatorial "giant of rivers." The year following, the species was found growing at White Haven, on the Lehigh River, Pennsylvania, (1000 ft. above the sea); in Lake Hopatcong, New Jersey, (alt. 1200 ft.); and was received from friends in several other parts of the country. My records show its receipt from at least eighteen different localities within eleven separate states, including the last arrival from Newfoundland. This specimen was peculiar, in so far as the larger rotules deviate from the ordinary rule of entire margins and are found divided into irregular rays or rounded segments. The smaller rotules are clearly rayed, and very irregular in size.

Generally speaking, the specimens gathered were filmy, indicating but a single years growth. At White Haven however, the fragments brought up by my "scraper net" from piling standing in deep water above the dam were, in some cases, a quarter inch or more in thickness; suggesting a serial growth somewhat like that of *Meyenia leidyi*.

The first records of this discovery describe the outer rotules as one fifth the diameter of the inner but varying in a few instances from this proportion to near equality. It required the experience of several years to convince me that, as, in specimens from different localities the prevailing proportions of the rotules differed in like manner, their relative sizes were no guides as to species. As a result of this teaching some names, given to supposed new species, must be ignored; including *T. fanshawei*, intended to honor a gentleman to whose courtesy I am indebted for the opportunity of making many of these explorations; and *T. intermedia*, supposed at one time to be a connecting link, but now known to be the species itself, in one of its multiform conditions.

Far up among the Pennsylvania mountains, fully 1800 feet above the sea, is Bear Lake, one of the sources of the Lehigh River. During a hurried hour or less spent upon it, one autumn day in 1883, we found, as its most characteristic feature, the rocks and rounded boulders in shallow water covered with a thin, light green sponge containing some gemmules. Repeated examinations, made after reaching home, showed it to be a *Tubella* of very delicate and fragile character as to its spicules, and exhibiting some peculiarities that I am not as yet prepared to describe. I have marked it

Tubella pennsylvanica, v. minima, Potts.

Sponge light green, encrusting, thin; texture loose and incoherent, sarcode having a granular appearance not fully understood.

Gemmules few; chitinous coat and granular crust both thin; the latter embedding a relatively very small number of inæquibirotulates.

Skeleton spicules slender, acuminate or somewhat rounded, entirely spined; spines perpendicular, cylindrical; terminations rounded.

Trumpet-shaped spicules with very slender, smooth, cylindrical, shafts, (in prepared specimens very generally broken); proximal rotules, large, flat or contorted; margins entire or more or less rayed; distal rotules hardly larger than the diameter of the shaft, too minute to detect any subdivisions.

After examining some slides of this variety I incidently turned to others of a form collected as an incrustation from some large water pipes, that had conveyed water from the Schuylkill River. The contrast was startling. The skeleton spicules here were short, robust and generally rounded; the birotulates also were very short, say one half the length of those last described; shafts thick and widening into each rotule. Rotulæ nearly equal in size, margins entire and both of them upturned, saucer-like; very closely resembling those of *M. leidyi*.

This was the major term of the series, and was reached after passing those from the 1800, the 1200, 1000 and 600 ft. altitudes; pausing first at 40 or 50 ft. above tide water, near Bristol, Pennsylvania, where, upon a mass of furnace slag, was found *T. fanshawei*, whose rotules bore the relation to each other of 5 to 6 or 6 to 7; then, in Indian Run, and still later, in tide water in the Schuylkill River below the dam, still greater robustness was reached and the rotulæ, found as above, were as nearly equal as those of *M. leidyi*.

The series was now complete from the last described form, back to that in which the outer rotule, and even the shaft itself, had been nearly eliminated; while the general features of the sponge, excepting as to robustness, remained the same. The changes, it will be observed, followed closely the lines of increasing altitude; their cause must be left for later determination.

The fact mentioned in the early part of my technical description, that specimens of this species are often seen, having their dermal surfaces covered with parallel-lying skeleton spicules, is well worthy of notice. A portion at least, of the skeleton spicules in all sponges seem to have their origin in this dermal film. If, under a high magnifying power, we watch the surface of a sponge that has germinated and is growing in a stage tank or other convenient receptacle, we will see these spicules carried about in the amœboid wanderings of the dermal cells, the end of each multiplying the motion and swaying like the gnomon of a time piece. Under these conditions they are probably prepared, and as the result of these motions they are placed to form the connecting links between the main lines of fasciculated spicules, that are themselves formed in the deeper parts of the sponge. In *T. pennsylvanica*, the spicules are short and slightly, if at all, fasciculated; and, as the crossing lines are more numerous, they require a greater proportion of these forms of *dermal* origin.

(V.) **Gen. PARMULA,** Carter. Ann. and Mag. 1881. p. 98.

Gen. char. Skeleton spicules nearly as in *Tubella*; generally robust, their ends rounded or abruptly terminated. Dermal spicules sometimes present. Gemmules surrounded by a granular or cellular crust of considerable thickness, charged with or embedding an armature of shield-shaped (parmuliform) spicules.

In the species of this genus, all from the River Amazon, South America, or from some of its tributaries, a further modification of the birotulate form of gemmule spicules may be observed. The outer rotule, that, in the last previous genus had become much inferior to the other, has now disappeared, as well as the larger portion of the shaft, leaving only the proximal rotule with an acuminate umbo, as a "scutulate" or "parmuliform" spicule.

Our first knowledge of the sponges pertaining to this genus, as well as of three of the Tubellas, already described, is derived from specimens collected by Mr. H. W. Bates during his sojourn upon the Amazon and its branches, from the year 1848 to 1859. His specimens appear to have been generally gathered in the neighborhood of Villa Nova, probably in a side channel of the main river; ("Dark Ygapos in virgin forest, margins of Amazons, Villa Nova.") On his return to England they were sent to Dr. Bowerbank, whose descriptions of them form the most interesting and valuable portions of his monograph.

In the far too meagre narrative that Mr. Bates has given us of his journeyings, ("The Naturalist on the River Amazons," London, John Murray, 1873.) we are informed that the changes of level in this portion of the river between the wet and dry seasons amount to 25 or even 35 feet; that the floods last from three to four months; and when the water retires "the trunks and lower branches of the trees are coated with dried slime, and disfigured by rounded masses of freshwater sponges, whose long horny spiculæ and dingy colors give them the appearance of hedge hogs."

It is rather remarkable that later travellers in this district do not seem to have had their curiosity excited by the singular appearance of these encrusting or suspended masses, so far as to induce them to collect specimens and bring them to the knowledge of specialists in this branch of science. Few if any, at least, are reported to have been seen or described, until now that a single specimen has fallen into my hands. It was collected during a transcontinental journey from the west coast of South America, through Bolivia and down the Beni, Madeira and Amazon Rivers, undertaken by Dr. H. H. Rusby, travelling in the interest of the enterprising drug firm of Parke, Davis & Co. of New York.

I failed to communicate with Dr. Rusby, as I had greatly desired, before he left the western side of the continent, to request his particular attention to these sponges; and the specimen referred to was one that only incidentally attracted his notice as he floated down the rivers. It was seen not in the water however, but hanging high and dry above it. When I had confirmed his supposition that it was a fresh water sponge, a species of *Parmula*, he wrote,—"It exists abundantly along the River Ibon a small branch of the Beni. When the river overflows, the sponge is deposited in the bushes. It is exactly spherical and of a size varying from that of a walnut to one foot in diameter. The spicules are poisonous when penetrating the flesh, producing a painful swelling that lasts for several days. It is said at times to produce lockjaw.[1] The overflow is annual and lasts only a few weeks. The sponge appears to vary in other localities in which I saw it. Beside this there are other quite different species that are deposited at the same time. One is a very dirty thing, like a mass of mud, or of mud mixed with ashes; of most irregular form, looking like the mud nests made by some species of ants and bees."

The principal specimen received from Dr. Rusby and probably the only species that he was aware that he collected, nearly resembles *Parmula brownii* (*S. brownii*, Bk.) and will be presently described

---

[1] I can say nothing confirmatory of the supposed poisonous character of these spicules, except what is probably already well known,—that when handling dried fresh water sponges of any kind, if the forehead, neck, wrists etc. are accidentally touched by the fingers, to which spicules may have adhered, the latter penetrate the skin and produce very perceptible and irritating welts which remain for several hours. I received recently from Mr. Henry L. Osborn of Lafayette, Indiana, a sample of fine dirt that was complained of by laborers who cultivated a certain field, as producing a greatly irritated condition of the skin in dry weather, when, as dust, it settled upon them. It appeared that a portion of this field had been an old "pond hole," since drained; and I found the dust to abound in the spicules of sponges that had once lived there.

as a variety of that species. Upon the slender stem that supports it however, on the two leaves pertaining to that stem and even parasitical amongst the spicules of the primary sponge, I discovered several other kinds; viz.—on the stem, little groups of *Meyenia gregaria* almost exactly as Dr. Bowerbank has described them;—on the leaves, *Spongilla navicella*, Carter, whose enigmatical character has been alluded to in the remarks on that species; also a curiously minute new species now described under the name of *Meyenia minuta*; and upon or within the sponge itself, a few gemmules of *Tubella recurvata* and many of a new species of *Parmula*, that will be presently noticed: six species belonging to four genera; with distinct but insufficient indications of one or two others. With a productiveness and withal a variety so great as this, it may not be cause of wonderment that the writer should feel that were the opportunity afforded thoroughly to examine a single log, that had floated for a year in one of the side channels of the Amazon, the history and classification of fresh-water sponges in America might have to be in large measure rewritten.

KEY TO THE SPECIES OF THE GENUS PARMULA.

1. Sponge rigid, coarsely reticulated. Gemmule surrounded by a tuberculated parenchyma, charged with parmuliform spicules, both upon the chitinous coat and on the outer surface of the tubercules, in which they are associated with a minute spined acerate. *P. batesii*.
2. Sponge rigid, coarsely reticulated. Crust of gemmules granular, penetrating the compact spicular capsule by many slender processes. No outer series of parmuliform spicules.
P. brownii.
3. Sponge minute; skeleton spicules not fasciculated. Crust of large granuliferous cells forming irregular rounded lobes whose size and shape are determined by the interspaces of the spicules of a much less compact capsule. No spined acerates. Parmuliform spicules forming a complete armature upon the chitinous coat. *P. rusbyi*.

The descriptions of the older species are copied from H. J. Carter, preferred to those of Dr. Bowerbank as showing the results of a later study of the specimens and one made in the light of the revised classification; yet in the course of my study of the same species I have been delighted with the minute accuracy of Dr. Bowerbank's observations, particularly those included in his general remarks.

(1) **Parmula batesii**, Carter. Ann. and Mag. 1881, p. 99.

Spongilla batesii, Bowerbank. Proc. Zool. Soc. 1863, p. 459.

Sponge "more or less globular when growing round the small immersed branches of trees one inch or more in thickness. Structure coarsely reticulate, extremely hard and rigid, rising into thorn-like processes on the surface. Color light sea-green. Skeleton spicule curved, fusiform, abruptly sharp-pointed, smooth, forming, when bundled together with the hard transparent sarcode, the rigid structure above mentioned, charged throughout with statoblasts. Statoblast large, globular, more or less uniformly tuberculated. Aperture infundibular. Crust very thick, composed of granular microcell-structure of a white color, which, growing out through the interstices of the reticular arrangement of skeleton-spicules, reduced in size, which form a capsular covering to the statoblast, gives it the tuberculated character mentioned. Charged with and surrounded by minute, thin, curved, fusiform, gradually sharp-pointed, spinous acerates, irregularly dispersed throughout its substance, limited, both inside and outside, by a layer of parmuliform spicules, the former in contact with the chitinous coat, and the latter on the free surface of the crust, giving it a light brown color. Parmuliform spicule circular, flat, infundibuliform, terminating in a point, like a little round shield turned up at the margin, which is even, arranged both internally and externally in juxtaposition, more or less overlapping each other, with the funnel-shaped process outwards in both instances, so that the surface of the crust is covered with little points."

Carter.

Loc. River Amazon.

(2) **Parmula brownii**, Carter. Ann. and Mag. 1881, p. 99.

Spongilla brownii, Bowerbank. Proc. Zool. Soc. 183, p. 457.

Sponge "globular four or more inches in diameter, appended to a small twig rather than embracing it. Structure and color the same as in the foregoing species. Skeleton-spicules the same but diminished to half their size round the statoblasts, to which they afford a distinct capsule. Statoblast globular; aperture slightly infundibular; crust thin, composed of microscopically minute, spherical cells, irregularly agglomerated together, so as to produce small lacinuliform processes, which project into the interspaces between the capsular spicules; unaccompanied by the spinous spicule, which is present in the foregoing species, and without a continuous layer of the parmuliform spicule over the surface, but presenting one in contact with the chitinous coat, where it is overlain by an extremely thin development of the microcellular crust, from which the lacinuliform processes above mentioned are projected." Carter.

Loc. British Guiana.

Parmula brownii, var. tuberculata, n. var.

Sponge as seen in a dried state, dark brown, massive, spherical; enveloping the small twig upon which it had grown. Mass extremely rigid, spinous at the superfices; reticulations many times larger than those of any known North American sponge. (The sarcode and dermis have now almost entirely disappeared.)

Gemmules numerous; granular crust rather thin, surrounded by a dense capsule of spicules, the interstices of which it penetrates by numerous fibre-like extensions, which, when seen in small white rounded prominences outside the capsule, give it a peculiar mottled appearance. The gemmules are firmly attached by their capsular spicules to the radiating and connecting lines of skeleton spicules *near* their outer extremities, and form a continuous zone just within the mass.

Skeleton spicules smooth, robust, nearly cylindrical, but slightly thicker at the middle; terminations abruptly pointed. Those of the capsule are similar, but about one half the length of the former and more curved. Many of them are covered with large and beautifully rounded tubercles which are the marked features of this variety.

Dermal spicules very minute, slender, spined acerates; spines at the middle long, perpendicular, rounded.

Gemmule spicules parmuliform or shield shaped; consisting of a subcircular proximal rotule with entire margin, then rapidly tapering into a central boss or spine whose length may be equal to one third or one half the diameter of the rotule. These are embedded under the crust resting upon the chitinous coat.

Hab. Upon trunks and branches of submerged trees.

Loc. Beni River, East Bolivia, S. A. Collected by Dr. H. H. Rusby.

The specimen of this variety of *P. brownii*, received from Dr. Rusby is about five inches in diameter, very rigid to the touch, but with meshes relatively very large, so that it was possible to see through the mass nearly at the centre. Its attachment to the twig around which it grew, is, at present, but slight, the twig having shrunken away from the primary supporting membrane. The radiating lines of skeleton spicules, slender at first, have gradually increased with the growth of the sponge, until, near their ends, their thickness may be that of 30 to 50 skeleton spicules *en fascicle*. In its living condition, of course, these lines of spicules were clothed with sarcode, and the outer surface, without doubt, was surrounded by a dermis of greater or less density, giving the sponge more the appearance of a solid mass than it has at present. The dermal spicules above described were found in some small patches of adherent brown substance, where they were associated with the proper skeleton and capsular spicules of this species and are therefore assumed to belong to it though not found *in situ*.

The gemmules are here a very interesting feature. Throughout the outer half inch of the mass, they are seen attached to every spicular thread, less like beads than grapes, and appear to have been formed at the close of the season of growth, or just before the retirement of the waters, left the sponge hanging in mid-air. It is of course important to learn, so far as may be possible from the examination of this specimen, whether the whole of the mass was formed during a single period of submergence. If not, I argue that another zone should be found within the first, formed at the termination of a previous season, the germination and colonial growth of whose gemmules would give rise to the "second story" of this structure. This appears to be the case. A spherical space of, say, one and a half inches diameter, at the centre of the mass, is charged with gemmules, while between this and the outer zone of gemmules, a space more than an inch in breadth is almost or entirely clear of them. It is supposable, therefore, that this specimen represents a growth of two years, at least of two seasons of submergence, and that the life of the sponge, whether it be in the condition of ova or of resting spores merely, has been preserved in the gemmules in despite of, say, eight or ten months of absolute desiccation.[1]

(3) **Parmula rusbyi**, n. sp.

Sponge minute, parasitic upon *P. brownii*, v. *tuberculata*; Spicules non-fasciculate. Mass, as seen, with no definite outline.

---

[1] After writing the above, it occurred to me to attempt the germination of some of the gemmules under consideration, and in one instance, within two days, and in another, in six hours after placing a few in water, an extrusion of germinal matter was observed. In neither case has this yet resulted in a recognizable embryonic sponge, but they sufficiently evidence continued vitality.

Gemmules numerous, without attachment, resting within open-meshed capsules, through which the crust expands itself in many large and irregularly rounded lobes, composed of large parenchymal cells filled with granular matter,[1] beneath which, in a single layer, the parmuliform spicules rest in a normal fashion upon the chitinous coat.

Skeleton spicules almost indistinguishable from those of the supporting species; their principal feature being, that they are loosely aggregated and never occur in bundles of fasciculated lines.

No dermal spicules seen.

Parmuliform gemmule spicules rest upon the chitinous coat, and from above them the parenchymal crust easily separates.

Hab. Only known within the meshes of *P. brownii*.

Loc. Beni River, etc. S. A.

The characteristic gemmules of this species (?) were first noticed among the debris of the above named variety. After an earnest effort to determine their origin and associations, they were at last traced to certain minute flocculent masses of indefinite shapes resting among the spicular lines of that sponge. The gemmules certainly differ in type from those of either of the before described species, and but one other solution occurs to me, besides that which I have adopted; viz. making it a new species; and this is, the possibility, barely a possibility, that they pertain to the principal sponge, as errant or floating gemmules, for the distribution of the species; as the more common and normal forms of *P. brownii* are so heavily weighted with capsular and skeleton spicules that when detached, they sink promptly to the depths of the water.

Pending the solution of this problem, I name it as a provisional species after Dr. Rusby, from whom science has received much and hopes for more.

(VI) Gen. CARTERIUS, Potts.

Carterella, Potts & Mills; Proc. Acad. Nat. Sci. 1881, p. 150.

Gen. Char. Skeleton spicules as in *Spongilla* or *Meyenia*. Gemmule globular, the chitinous coat around the foraminal aperture

---

[1] A re examination of several mounted specimens of *P. rusbyi*, made with a view to affirm or disprove certain suggestions of my friend Carter, has convinced me that the *granular matter*, above spoken of in this and probably also in other cases, differs from that condition of the crust that has been called *cellular* in no other respect than in the *size* of the cells. The large parenchymal cells in this case, therefore, contain within them or are subdivided into, immense numbers of the smaller kind. It should be said that Mr. Carter prefers to consider this a mere variety of *P. brownii.*

expanded and prolonged into a tube of variable length in the different species, whose termination is either funnel-shaped, disk-like with fibrous margins, or divided into one or several cirrous appendages sometimes of considerable relative length, curling or twisting about each other or surrounding objects. Birotulate spicules akin to those of *Meyenia* or *Hetromeyenia*. (Pl. VI, figs. iii, iv, v and vi.)

The name *Carterella* was first applied to this genus in June 1881, at the suggestion of Mr. (now Prof.) Jno. A. Ryder, in honor of my friend H. J. Carter, Esq. F. R. S. etc. whose scientific life, more than that of any other man had been devoted to the study of the marine and fresh water sponges. During the previous summer two species possessing the features indicated had been discovered by Mr. Mills of Buffalo and myself, and briefly described as of the genus *Spongilla*, which had not then been divided. The approval of Mr. Mills was courteously given to the use of the name *Carterella*, which, a few years later was necessarily changed to *Carterius*, on the discovery that the former term had been preoccupied by Zittel in the same association, to designate one of his fossil types. At that time and for several years after, the occurrence of cirrous appendages was altogether unknown among European sponges; but the past few years, which have been so fruitful of American species in foreign parts, have developed one of this type in Russia, and later, in Bohemia, called by its discoverer, Dr. W. Dybowski, *Dosilia stepanowii*.

The tendrils of the three recognized American species, *C. tubisperma*, *C. latitenta* and *C. tenosperma*, differ obviously in length and character, and with the Russian species probably present as many types of these organic features, as it will be profitable to designate by specific names. Several intermediate forms have, however, been noticed by Mr. Mills and B. W. Thomas Esq., of Chicago, varying as to the length of the foraminal tubules and the character of the supported tendrils; the most noticeable case, being the substitution of a flaring funnel-shaped termination of the tubule, for the latter organs.

KEY TO THE SPECIES OF THE GENUS CARTERIUS.

1. Foraminal tubule terminating in a sub-quadrangular disk at whose angles the chitin divides into processes of variable length. (Pl. VI, fig. iv.)   *C. (Dosilia) stepanowii*.
2. Foraminal tubule very long and slender; tendrils short, irregular, or wavering. (Pl. VI, fig. iii.)   *C. tubisperma*.

3. Foraminal tubule shorter; tendrils one or two, enveloping the tubule. (Pl. VI, fig. v.) *C. latitenta.*

4. Foraminal tubule still shorter; tendrils three to five, very long and slender. (Pl. VI, fig. vi.) *C. tenosperma.*

(1) **Carterius stepanowii**, Petr. (Pl. VI, fig. iv.)

Dosilia stepanowii, Dybowski. 1884. See Vejdovsky, "Diagnosis" etc., p. 179.

In reference to this species, described as above by Prof. Vejdovsky, I am kindly permitted to make use of the following note by H. J. Carter, F. R. S. etc. in Ann. and Mag. Nat. Hist. 1887, p. 212.

"This fresh-water sponge, which in 1884 was named "*Dosilia* (?) *stepanowii* by Dr. W. Dybowski, from a specimen found near Charkow, in southern Russia (Annals, 1884, Vol. XIV. p. 60), was also found in 1885 by Prof. Fr. Petr, of the University of Prague, in the neighborhood of Deutschbrod, in Bohemia, about 60 miles South East of that city; and his description of it, which is beautifully illustrated, was published in the Czech language at Prague, in 1886. It appears to be the same as that discovered by Mr. H. Mills, of Buffalo, New York, in the Niagara River, in 1880, viz: *Carterius tubisperma* (Proc. Acad. Nat. Sci. Philadelphia, 14th. June, 1881, p. 150).

"Thus this remarkable genus of *Spongilla*, first brought to notice by Mr. Ed. Potts, of Philadelphia, in a specimen found in a small stream in the late Centennial grounds, Fairmount Park, Philadelphia (*ib.* about August, 1880,) which he then named *S. tentasperma*, and subsequently *S. tenosperma* (*ib.* p. 357), ending with *Carterius tenosperma*, its present name, has now been found in Southern Russia and mid-Europe, as above stated.

"In the same communication also Prof. Petr has described and illustrated, under the provisional name of *Ephydatia bohemica*, another fresh-water sponge, found at Kavasetice, in the same district, wherein the statoblast presents an incipient condition of the curious development characterizing *Carterius*, with a spiculation which appears to me, from the illustrations, to be very like that of his *C. stepanowii*.

"Lastly, Mr. H. Mills of Buffalo, in a letter dated 20th. Nov. 1886, sent me a specimen of *Carterius* from the Niagara River which he considers allied to *C. latitenta*, Potts, wherein the expanded portion of this development presents itself under the form of a cup, with even, circular margin, (that is entirely without cirrous appendages), whose bottom is pierced by the upright tubular part in the usual way; which "form" appears to prevail generally in the statoblasts of this variety."

2) **Carterius tubisperma**, Mills. Proc. Acad. Nat. Sci. June 1881, p. 150. (Pl. VI, fig. iii.)

Spongilla——Mills. Am. Jour. Micros. June 1880, p. 132.

Sponge brown or green, massive, loose textured; surface wavelike.

Gemmulæ numerous, spherical, relatively large; crust charged with birotulate spicules. Foraminal apertures prolonged into slender, cylindrical tubes, whose greatest length is about equal to the diameter of the gemmule, abruptly flaring at their terminations into several short, inconsequent tendrils of less or greater length. (Pl. VI, fig. iii, a.)

Skeleton spicules rather slender, fasciculate, subfusiform, gradually pointed, sparsely spiniferous; spines small, rounded. (Pl. XII, fig. vi, a.a.)

Dermal spicules long, slender, acerates; generally straight, entirely spined; spines near the middle of the spicules long, cylindrical; terminations rounded. (Ibid. c.c.)

Gemmule birotulates abundant, irregular in length, (suggesting the genus *Hetromeyenia*); shafts cylindrical, sometimes with one or more spines; outer surface of rotules arched; rays numerous, long; terminations incurved (ibid. b.b.b.c.)

Meas. Skeleton spicules 0·0099 by 0·00025 inches. Dermal spicules 0·0038 inches long. Birotulates 0·0019 by 0·00015 inches. Diameter of disk 0·0008 inches.

Hab. On timbers etc.

Loc. Niagara River, New York; Cochituate Reservoir, Boston, Mass. etc.

The original description by Mr. Mills of his species, given as above in June 1880, without specific name is as follows :—

"Sponge low, branching (?) green, growing on the upper surface of stones in not very deep water. Skeleton spiculæ fusiform-acerate, slightly arcuate, moderately stout, spined; spines small, sparsely distributed; length 0·01 to 0·012 inches, apices naked. These are mixed with a great many fine delicate spicula (dermals) densely spined to the end; length 0·009 inches, scattered in groups on each slide of mounted specimens. Ovaria globose; diameter 0·02 inches. Foramen tubed; tube terminating with five (?) finger-like processes somewhat resembling tentacles. Spicula birotulate, long, very delicate; length of axle 0·0015 inches, one or more large spines on each axle. Rotulæ slightly arcuate, equal in size. Length of tube to foramen 0·01 inches. Length of tentacle shaped processes, one fiftieth to one eightieth of an inch."

(3) **Carterius latitenta**, Potts. Proc. Acad. Nat. Sci. Phila. July 1881, p. 176. (Pl. VI, fig. v,. Pl. XII, fig. v.)

Sponge green, encrusting stones etc.; texture very loose; the longer bands of skeleton spicules rising into abrupt wave-lines at short distances; masses thicker near the middle.

Gemmulæ numerous, spherical; crust charged with birotulate spicules; foramina prolonged into tapering (narrowing) tubules shorter than those of *C. tubisperma*; terminations rounded. Cirrous appendages, at first flat and ribbon-like, enveloping the tubule, (or pierced by it), some distance below its termination; frequently but one, rarely more than two of these, which soon become slender and rounded, long and tapering, occasionally subdividing into many short irregular ones. (Pl. VI, fig. v. a. and d.)

Skeleton spicules fusiform, smooth or very sparsely microspined, gradually pointed. (Pl. XII, fig. v. a.a.)

Dermal spicules long, acerate, slightly curved, entirely spined; spines irregular, longer towards the middle of the spicule. (Ibid. c.c.)

Birotulate spicules stout; shafts with numerous long, pointed spines; surfaces of rotules rounded; rays deeply cut, tapering, sometimes incurved (ibid. b.b.b.d.) (Pl. VI, fig. v. b.)

Meas. Skeleton spicules 0·0111 by 0·00045 inches. Length of dermal spicules 0·0038 inches. Birotulates 0·0019 by 0·00015 inches. Diameter of disk 0·001 inches.

Hab. On stones etc., in rapidly running water.

Loc. Chester Creek, Pennsylvania; Western New York etc.

In the summer of 1881, I resided temporarily in a fine agricultural district in Chester County, Pennsylvania. As a rule, July is, in this part of the world, too early for the collection of mature specimens. Some species, however, form their gemmules thus early; and, while wading along the east branch of Chester Creek, there a shallow stream, averaging eight or ten feet in width, turning over stones in the "riffs," or little rapids, probing the roots of encroaching trees and examining the stems of water plants, I found traces of a sponge, which, under the microscope, proved to be a third species of

Carterius. The gemmules were young, to be sure, but the tendrils were there and the novelty of the species was easily seen.

Further down the stream, where the public road crosses it by an old-fashioned "covered-bridge," in the shelter of it and, incidentally, protected from the trampling of cattle by fences of barbed wire, was found the very headquarters, the "zoological garden" of this species. Nearly every stone and the gravelly bed of the stream between them, was covered with it just under the surface of the water. The masses were not large, say five or six inches in diameter; and while thickest near the middle, tapered off into a delicate nimbus around the edges. This appearance was more conspicuous during the early autumn, when, the thicker portions having become brown with age, a new growth, probably from the germination of some of the older gemmules, had started around the edges, and in this no gemmules could yet be found. Soon after, the bunches began to dwindle in size, and on the day after Christmas of that year, I find it recorded, "the *masses* have all been washed away, leaving a slight muddy incrustation, consisting partially of filiform algæ, with numerous sponge gemmules and their tendrils, which have aided in binding the particles of a deposit of silt or fine mud into a persistent film, that will probably last until the time for germination next spring." The following year the amount of this sponge, in that locality, was much reduced, and since that date I have had no opportunity to examine it.

In common with the other two species, this fresh-water sponge is very loosely held together; with the same conspicuous wave-lines of spicules marking its surface. On the gemmules, the broad ribbon-like tendrils, seemingly pierced by the tapering ends of the foraminal tubules, are in strong contrast with the slender, thread-like filaments of *C. tenosperma*, next to be described; still less do they resemble those inconsequent, almost embryonic, features of *C. tubisperma* and *C. (Dosilia) stepanowii.* Yet the spicules of this species, skeleton, dermal and birotulate, closely resemble those of *C. tubisperma* and both are suggestive of *H. repens.*

(4) **Carterius tenosperma,** Potts. (Pl. VI, fig. vi; Pl. XII. fig. iv.)

Spongilla tentasperma, Potts. Proc. Acad. Nat. Sci. Phila. July 1880.

Spongilla tenosperma, Potts. Proc. Acad. Nat. Sci. Phila. Nov. 1880, p. 357.

Carterella tenosperma, Potts. Proc. Acad. Nat. Sci. Phila. June 1881, p. 150.

Sponge yellowish-green; creeping upon and around water-plants and roots, matting them together and thus forming loose, irregular masses several inches in diameter, often including shells of *Planorbis* and other snails. Less frequently it is found encrusting the upper surface of stones or the gravelly bed of a stream to the depth of two or three lines. Sponge itself of no describable form.

Gemmulæ spherical, light yellow or brown, rather numerous among the skeleton spiculæ and the attached roots; granular crust charged with birotulate spicules. Foramina sub-elliptically enlarged and prolonged to a length about equal to one fourth the diameter of the gemmule. Just below its rounded termination it gradually flares and divides into two to five tapering, slender, curling or twisted tendrils, whose length may be as much as a half an inch. These cirrous appendages or prolongations of the chitinous coat of the gemmule in this species are generally round, but occasionally, near their origin, are flat for a short distance. (Pl. VI, fig. vi.)

Skeleton spicules slender, subfusiform, gradually pointed, very sparsely microspined. (Pl. XII, fig. iv. a.a.)

Dermal spicules slender, nearly straight acerates, entirely spined; spines longer near the middle of the spicules. (Ibid. d.d.d.)

Birotulate spicules with cylindrical shafts, abundantly spined; spines as long as the rays of the rotules; acutely conical. Rays of supposable rotules numerous, spreading outward like a burr or brush; often with a spinous prolongation in the line of the shaft. (Ibid. b. b. c.c. c.c.)

Meas. Skeleton spicules 0·0098 by 0·00025 inches. Length of dermal spicules 0·0028 inches. Birotulate spicules 0·0018 by 0·0001 inches. Diameter of disk 0·0006 inches.

Hab. As described.

Loc. Lansdowne Run, Centennial Grounds, Philadelphia; Lehigh River, Bethlehem, Pennsylvania; Rahway River, New Jersey, etc.

The visitor to the American Centennial Exposition of 1876, whether foreigner or "to the manner born," if but for a minute he withdrew his eyes from that wonderful display of human art and rested them upon the natural beauties of the landscape in the midst of which it was placed, can hardly even now fail to remember the "Lake" with its ever flowing geyser fountain, lying north of "Machinery Hall." Escaping by a passage under the "Belmont Road," the overflow of this pond made its way to the Schuylkill River through the lovely "Lansdowne Glen," filling the little "Run" that, before and since that summer, has but softly murmured through it, with an unfamiliar turmoil of waters. In its normal condition this stream is one a child could step over at almost any point, and all its water could probably be carried through a six-inch pipe.

That portion of it just below Belmont Avenue has become somewhat famous in our local biological annals. It was here that Prof. Leidy found, a year or two after the "Centennial," thousands of colonies of his beautiful Bryozoan, *Cristatella idæ*, covering every stick and stone. Here in 1878 the writer discovered that fragment of *Spongilla fragilis*, which, thus accidentally, directed his attention toward a line of study in which he has since had such great enjoyment; and here two years later was first found the subject of the present memoir, a sponge whose novelty was exhibited in a greater departure from previously known types, than had been the case with any before discovered. *Spongilla tentasperma, S. tenosperma, Carterella tenosperma* and *Carterius tenosperma*, ring the changes in its name and history, till it now stands accepted, I trust, (coincidently with *C. tubisperma* of Mr. Mills,) as the first instance in which the spherical chitinous body of a sponge gemmule has attained a cirrous development, conspicuous in its character and evident in its purpose.

The cirri in this species are very long and slender; curling and twisting in infinite contortions about themselves and the roots among which they grow;—so long, that they have been combed out to an actual length of half an inch, or twenty five times the diameter of the gemmules of which they are parts. More or less of the sponge was found at the same locality for several successive years, until 1885, when, as search was not made until December, its apparent absence was not to be wondered at.

One circumstance not easily explained must be mentioned as a part of its history. The birotulates of those gemmulæ collected in 1880 were peculiar in this,—there were no proper rotules, and the rays at the ends of each spicule stood out in every direction, like the bristles of a mop. On those gathered during the following, and, so far as I remember, during subsequent years, this habit has changed and the rotules in nearly all cases are perfect. The collections were made at precisely the same locality; and in all other respects the sponges appear to be identical.

We have now examined in detail all the genera comprised in the group *Spongillina*, that are clearly characterized by the presence of "seed-like reproductive organs called statoblasts" or gemmules. There yet remain three genera in which no such organs have been discovered. As shown by their geographical derivation, they are as certainly *fresh water sponges* as any of the others, and the absence of the supposed distinctive features, may or may not prove to be real. They have *not yet* been found; that is all. But neither have the sponges been examined at the place of their growth, if we except the *Lubomirskiæ*, by any one familiar with the peculiarities of the fresh water forms, who has torn to pieces mass after mass, as was done in the case of *S. lacustris*, v. *abortiva*, *S. aspinosa*, *H. pictovensis* etc; as must be done in our treatment of all the evergreen sponges, which, probably for the very reason that they live throughout the year, perfect but few gemmules.

I know that it is in the line of my own arguments, already given, to believe it possible that fresh water sponges, living in deep, tropical waters, should not adopt this method of reproduction; and I *do* believe it, *theoretically*. It is necessary however that this theory should be proved by a more thorough and systematic examination, of the genera now to be briefly mentioned, which are neither all tropical nor "deep" in their origin, when, if they maintain their claim, it will be in order to form a new group to comprise them.

Between two of these genera there is a strong family resemblance at least in the forms of their skeleton spicules. Those of the third genus, *Lubomirskia*, as well as the prevailing habit of the species, seem to differ from the others. I regret that I have not been able to find English translations of Dr. Dybowski's descriptions, but can present only the meagre sketches prepared by H. J. Carter from his examination of the plates furnished by the author.

(VIIa.) **Prov. Gen. URUGUAYA**, Carter.

Urugnaya corallioides, Carter. Ann. and Mag. 1881, p. 100.

Spongilla corallioides, Bowerbank. Proc. Zool. Soc. etc. 1863, p. 460.

Sponge "irregularly digitate; rising into a polychotomous and anastomosing mass of cylindrical branches, which may attain several inches (seven or more) in all directions. Color faint whitish yellow or dark leaden on the surface; internally white or colorless.

Surface even, vitreous in appearance, extremely hard, smooth and compact, interrupted by small raised vents, more or less uniformly distributed at short and unequal distances from each other. Internal structure composed of short, densely reticulated fibre, formed of the skeleton spicules of the sponge, in bundles firmly united together by colorless sarcode, which, together with the spicules, in a dried state, simulates, from its hardness and vitreous appearance an *entirely* silicified mass. Skeleton-spicule very robust, much curved, cylindrical, rounded at both ends, smooth or microspined, about six times longer than it is broad. Statoblast unknown." Carter.

Loc. "Rapids of the River Uruguay, above the town of Salto, Uruguay."

Several large specimens of this sponge have been collected by different travellers, and are deposited in English museums. Mr. Carter mentions the names of Messrs. George Higgin, W. Bragge, R. M. Andrew, and Dr. Garland in this connection.

(VII b.) Gen. **POTAMOLEPIS**, Marshall.

Zeit. fur Naturwissenchaft, XVI. N. F.IX. Bd. 553. Leipzig, May, 1883.

"Monactinellid, silicious, fresh-water sponges of great brittleness, with curved, obtuse, smooth spicules, which, when dry, are closely cemented together by a small quantity of organic substance. No gemmules." Marshall.

The descriptions of the following species, are abbreviated from a translation of the above paper, as found in the "Ann. and Mag." etc. 1883, p. 391 etc. The specimens examined and described by Dr. Wm. Marshall were collected by Dr. Pechuël-Loesche from the Congo River, Africa, about 150 miles from the sea, and above several "Falls" named.

(1) **Potamolepis leubnitziæ**, Marshall.

"Forming crusts of 1-1·5 millim. thick, finely porous, of yellowish white color and silky lustre ; exactly the appearance of unbaked wafers. The surface presents a few crateriform elevations of 0·25-0·40 mm. in height, standing in not very distinctly marked rows, upon faint undulations, which divide dichotomously in both directions and frequently disappear, and in which a certain parallelism is unmistakeable. At the summit of each elevation there is an osculum of irregular elongati-ovate and sometimes elongati-triangular or pentagonal form, separated usually by a space of two millimeters. The mouths, which are usually furnished not with smooth but with finely notched margins, lead into shallow gastric spaces, which immediately break up into several canals ; in the *angular* mouths a canal is frequently found at each angle." "These canals run horizontally, branching dichotomously and communicating with those pertaining to the neighboring oscular systems. Incurrent apertures numerous, circular, about 0·1 mm. in diameter, though some are much smaller."

(2) **Potamolepis chartaria,** Marshall.

"Oral cone isolated with round, *entire* margins 0·8–1 mm. in diameter. Incurrent apertures not numerous, 0·1 mm. in breadth. Surface like blotting paper, with a dermal skeleton composed of very delicate, felted, straight acerates 0·08 mm. long. Color of sponge when dry, chocolate-brown."

(3) **Potamolepis pechuëlii,** Marshall.

"Sponge crust-like, with numerous oscular cones 10 mm. high, oval at base; the longer and shorter diameters being about as 2 to 1. These cones are placed in rows in the direction of their longest diameters and are generally inclined at an angle of about 45°. The spicules of the species are more slender and less bent than those of either of the others. The color of the sponge is ash-gray with a silky lustre, and this and the large size of the meshes give it the appearance of coarsely porous pumice-stone." Marshall, abridged.

As before remarked, the skeleton spicules throughout this genus closely resemble those of Uruguaya; both being stout, cylindrical, curved, with hemispherical terminations. I understand Mr. Marshall to say that he would probably have attached his species to Mr. Carter's genus if its title had not been so "inconveniently local."

The reader is referred to Dr. Marshall's paper on these Congo sponges, for many interesting and valuable observations.

(VIIc.) Gen. **LUBOMIRSKIA**?

(1) **Lubomirskia baicalensis,** Pallas.

Mr. Carter remarks: "One learns from the figure of this species, that it consisted of long digital processes, about 14 inches long by one half an inch in their greatest diameter; more or less uniformly inflated at short intervals (that is, bullate), but solid throughout. (Dr. Marshall remarks that specimens have been found 60 centimeters, nearly 24 inches, high.) Structure elastic, but not crumbling between the fingers. Color dark gray or olive green. Skeleton spicule curved, fusiform, gradually sharp pointed, spiniferous generally, but especially towards the ends, while in some cases the rest of the shaft is smooth. Parenchyma spicule a smooth, thin acerate."

Carter.

Loc. Lake Baikal, Central Asia.

(2) **Lubomirskia bacillifera,** Dybowski.

Sponge "massive, more or less lobed. Structure much the same as that of the foregoing species, but finer and softer. Color grass-green. Skeleton spicule curved, cylindrical, sometimes fusiform, round at the ends, and spiniferous generally, but more particularly over the ends; sometimes smooth over the rest or middle of the shaft. Parenchyma spicule a small, thin, smooth acerate." Carter.

Loc. Lake Baikal.

(3) **Lubomirskia intermedia,** Dybowski.

Sponge "flat, spreading. Structure like that of *L. baicalensis*, but more tender. Color yellowish or olive-green. Skeleton-spicule curved, fusiform, gradually sharp-pointed, spiniferous generally. Parenchyma spicule a large, smooth acerate." Carter.

Loc. Lake Baikal.

(4) **Lubomirskia papyracea,** Dybowski.

Sponge "papyraceous in thinness, with smooth, shining surface. Structure very soft. Color white. Skeleton thick, (seven times longer than broad), curved, cylindrical, round at the ends, thickly spiniferous throughout. Parenchyma spicule a very small, smooth acerate." Carter.

The above species, described by Dr. W. Dybowski, were collected by his brother Dr. Benedict Dybowski and Herr W. Godleuski, all from Lake Baikal in Siberia. Very many specimens were obtained by them from various depths in the Lake, and the conclusion reached by their intelligent observations was that the sponge was totally devoid of gemmules. I do not know that these observations sufficiently covered the range of the seasons, to make the result positive. The condition of Lake Baikal as a geologically "recent" fresh-water lake, still retaining in its fauna etc., traces of its former marine character, (such as the existence of seals in it or in a recently connected body of water), renders these observations peculiarly important.

CONCLUSION.

In closing this (third) Monograph of the fresh-water sponges, it is with the consciousness that the work of classification occupies a very humble place among biological efforts and that all systems must of necessity be tentative and temporary, soon to be superseded by others, the results of a larger knowledge, gained by the contemplation of a wider horizon. Even so, it has its value in helping forward this very result.

Some points in the present seemingly narrow field of scientfic labor, worthy of the thought and study of future students have already been suggested, such as the *necessity* of gemmules in fresh water as distinguished from marine sponges; the process of their formation; their function and the means by which that end is attained; the law of variation in the quantity and character of the enveloping crust, and the time and mode of formation of the embedded armature;—all have yet to be conclusively studied. Other questions of a more limited character occur, in the search for the line of derivation that must be supposed to run through all the genera and species; and in the association, apparently indicated amongst otherwise dissimilar species, by the presence in them of correspondent forms, such as the birotulate dermals found in certain Spongillas and Meyenias and the more frequent recurrence in several genera, of acerate dermals with characteristic, centrally located, perpendicular spines, etc.

The true meaning of such facts must yet be discovered, and I know of no more hopeful field of labor for a young naturalist, seeking for "new worlds to conquer," than that provided by the fresh-water sponges. The few active workers in this field, in North America, have, thus far, but glanced at a few streams and lakes, mostly in the neighborhoods of Buffalo, Chicago and Philadelphia, and in parts of Florida, Nova Scotia and Newfoundland. There can be little doubt that the rest of the Continent holds many rare prizes in trust for younger and better equipped explorers.

EXPLANATION OF PLATES.

The magnification used in plates V. and VI. is irregular, as suited the several subjects of the artist. The figures on plates VII to XII inclusive, are uniformly magnified about 200 times and represent the spicules as seen upon prepared slides.

PLATE V.

Fig. I. *Spongilla lacustris.* Surface of gemmule showing,–*a*, position and character of "infundibular" foraminal aperture; *b*, acerate gemmule spicules, lying upon, or imbedded in, a granular "crust." (See Pl. VII.) The position of these greatly varies in the different "varieties" or "forms," governed generally by the thickness of said "crust."

Fig. II. *Spongilla fragilis.* • *A*, upper surface of part of "pavement layer" of gemmules; *a*, foraminal tubules, mostly curved, located at the centre of the upper surface of each gemmule; *b,b*, *acerate* spicules embedded in the "cellular parenchyma" which surrounds and combines the gemmules. (See Pl. VIII.) *B*, section of "group" of "errant" gemmules; *a*, curved foraminal tubules, *always outward;* *b*, envelope of cellular parenchyma charged with acerate spicules.

Fig. III. *Spongilla igloviformis.* *A*, "elevation" of dome-shaped group of gemmules, showing through the surface of the "cellular parenchyma" which has been made transparent, the several gemmules in position, surrounded by the echinating *acerate* "parenchyma spicules." (Pl. VIII, fig. v.) *B*, the surface (transparent) of a similar group as seen from above. The foraminal apertures, not here visible, all open *inward*.

Fig. IV. *Meyenia leidyi.* *A*, upper surface of portion of a layer of gemmules, each of which, besides its *"birotulate"* armature, (Pl. X, fig. i.) (not shown in this sketch) is surrounded by–*c*, a "lattice capsule" of spicules resembling those of the skeleton; at the summit of which an open space occurs, around–*a*, the foraminal aperture; more than one being sometimes present. *B*, section of part of "chitinous coat" of a gemmule, showing (imperfectly)–*b*, its armature of *birotulate* spicules in position.

Fig. V. *Meyenia fluviatilis.* Surface of gemmule. "Crust" charged with "*birotulate*" spicules (amphidisks); one star-shaped "rotule" resting upon the chitinous coat, the other presented to the observer, or more or less foreshortened. (See Pl. IX, fig. iii, etc.)

Fig. VI. *Meyenia crateriformis.* Section of chitinous coat of gemmule, supporting–*b*, hooked "birotulates" with very long shafts; whose positions, normally radial, are, in this species, frequently twisted or confused. (Pl. X, fig. v.)

Plate VI.

Fig. I. *Heteromeyenia argyrosperma.* Partial section of "chitinous coat" and "crust" of gemmule, showing:—*a*, the somewhat narrowing "foraminal aperture;" thick "granular crust" charged with–*b*, "long" and–*b¹*, "short" *birotulate* spicules. (Pl. XI, fig. i and ii.) The outer rotules of the longer birotulates, when covered by the crust, form conical protuberances as figured. They are, perhaps, more frequently seen naked.

Fig. II. *Tubella pennsylvanica.* Partial section of chitinous coat of gemmule, surrounded with granular crust; in which are embedded,–*b*, minute, *inæquibirotulate* spicules, (Pl. XII, fig. i, ii, iii.) the larger rotule always resting upon the chitinous coat. The thickness of the "crust," in this species, varies in different localities, from barely equalling the height of the spicules, to the extreme of covering them two or more times that depth.

Fig. III. *Carterius tubisperma.* Partial section of chitinous coat and crust of gemmule; the latter embedding–*b*, birotulate-spicules. Foraminal aperture prolonged into a long tubule–*a*, flaring and funnel-shaped at its extremity and divided into several short tendrils or cirrous appendages,–*d*.

Fig. IV. *Carterius stepanowii.* Partial section of gemmule showing protoplasmic contents, crust, birotulate spicules–*b*, foraminal tubule–*a*, penetrating the subquadrangular, flange-like extension–*d*, divided at the angles into numerous very short cirrous appendages. (after Dybowski.)

Fig. V. *Carterius latitenta.* Partial section of chitinous coat, bearing crust, and birotulate spicules–*b*; and extended into a foraminal tubule shorter than that of either of the previous species, surrounded and terminated by one or two long and broad, ribbon-like cirrous appendages–*d*.

Fig. VI. *Carterius tenosperma*. Section as before; the short tubule –*a*, divided into several long, slender cirrous appendages–*d*.

Plate VII.

Fig. I. *Spongilla lacustris*. From an Ice Lake, on the Sierra Nevada Mts, alt. 7000 feet:–*a*, skeleton spicule; *b,b,b* bent, cylindrical, *acerate* gemmule spicules; *c,c,c*, spined acerate "dermal" or flesh spicules. Received from Dr. H. W. Harkness, through Miss. M. M. Greer.

Fig. II. *Spongilla lacustris*. From Ridley Creek, near Media, Pennsylvania:–*a,a*, skeleton spicules; *b,b,b*, *acerate* gemmule spicules; *c,c,c*, "dermal" acerates.

Fig. III. *Spongilla lacustris*. From English type, received from H. J. Carter:–*a,a,a*, skeleton spicules; *b,b*, etc. *acerate* gemmule spicules; *c,c*, dermal acerates.

Fig. IV. *Spongilla lacustris*. From May's Landing, New Jersey: –*a,a,a*, skeleton spicules; *b,b*, long, spinous, *acerate* gemmule spicules; *c,c*, small dermal acerates.

Fig. V. *Spongilla lacustris*, var. *lehighensis*. From the Lehigh River, at White Haven, Pennsylvania:–*a,a*, skeleton spicules; *b, b, b*, strongly spinous gemmule spicules; *c,c,c,c*, short dermal acerates.

Fig. VI. *Spongilla lacustris*, var. *montana*. From Lake on Catskill Mts., New York, alt. 2500 feet; representing skeleton and gemmule spicules; no dermals have been drawn.

Plate VIII.

Fig. I. *Spongilla fragilis*. From *type specimen* "presented by Dr. Jos. Leidy to the Academy of Natural Sciences, Philadelphia:"–*a,a,a,a*, skeleton spicules; *b,b,b,b*, spicules from the "cellular parenchyma."

Fig. II. *Spongilla fragilis*, var. *minutissima*. From Lake Hopatcong, New Jersey:–*a,a*, skeleton spicules; *b,b*, spined forms sometimes seen; *c,c,c*, long, irregular, spinous parenchymal spicules.

Fig. III. *Spongilla fragilis.* From Calumet River, Illinois:—*a,a*, skeleton spicules; *b, c, d, e*, variable parenchymal spicules; *f,f,f*, spined, spherical forms frequently seen throughout the species. Collected by B. W. Thomas.

Fig. IV. *Spongilla fragilis*, var. *minuta.* From Lehigh Gap, Pennsylvania:—*a,a,a*, skeleton spicules; *b,b,b*, long, spined, acuminate, "parenchymal spicules;" *c,c,c*, spherical and amorphous forms.

Fig. V. *Spongilla igloviformis.* From Doughty's Pond, Absecum, New Jersey:—*a, a, c*, skeleton spicules; *b,b*, "parenchymal spicules" nearly equally long, but more spinous.

Fig. VI. *Spongilla aspinosa.* From Doughty's Pond, Absecum, New Jersey:—*a*, ordinary skeleton spicule; *b*, skeleton spicule; *acuate* or rounded at one end; *c, d*, malformations of skeleton spicules; *e,e,e*, smooth dermal spicules; *f,f,f*, globular or discoidal masses of silica, frequently observed in this species.

PLATE IX.

Fig. I. *Meyenia fluviatilis.* From an English type, received from H. J. Carter:—*a* and *b*, spined skeleton spicules; *c*, smooth do.; *d,d,d*, birotulate gemmule spicules sometimes with acuminate umbos; *e,e,e*, end view of rotules.

Fig. II. *Meyenia fluviatilis* var. *acuminata.* From Boston, Massachusetts:—*a*, ordinary skeleton spicule; *b,b*, slender forms of do.; *c,e,d,d*, acuminate or misshapen birotulate gemmule spicules.

Fig. III. *Meyenia fluviatilis*, form *astrosperma*, syn. From Lehigh Gap, Pennsylvania:—*a,a*, skeleton spicules; *b,b*, birotulate gemmule spicules; *d,d*, malformed do.; *c*, group of rotulæ; *e,e*, single rotules showing an ordinary distribution of the rays.

Fig. IV. *Meyenia fluviatilis.* From Chester Creek, near Lenni, Pennsylvania:—*a*, proper skeleton spicule; *b*, malformed do.; *d,d,d*, short, robust birotulates; *c,c,c* rotules with symmetrical, conical rays, sub-spined at margins; *e,e,e,e*, malformations of birotulates, frequent in this specimen.

Fig. V. *Meyenia robusta.* From Honey Lake Valley, California;—*a, a*, smooth skeleton spicules; *b,b,b*, coarsely spined gemmule birotulates; d,d,d, single rotules; e,e,e,e, exceedingly misshapen forms. Collected by Dr. Geo. H. Horn.

Fig. VI. *Meyenia subdivisa.* From St. John's River, near Palatka, Florida:–a, smooth, b, c, d, spined skeleton spicules; e,e, e,e, long, massive gemmule birotulates, spined and subspined; f,f, rotules of do. Collected by Henry Mills.

PLATE X.

Fig. I. *Meyenia leidyi.* From Schuylkill River, Philadelphia, Pennsylvania:–a,a,a, smooth skeleton spicules, abruptly pointed; b,b, do. with rounded terminations; c,c, short birotulates with "entire" margins; d, do. with rotule twisted or exflected; e, face of rotule; f, group of rotules as they appear upon the surface of the gemmules.

Fig. II. *Meyenia millsii.* From Florida:–a, microspined skeleton spicule; b,b, mature gemmule birotulates with smooth shafts; c,c,c, probably immature forms; d,d,d, face of rotules, "laciniulate" or delicately notched, and without rays. Collected by H. Mills;

Fig. III. *Meyenia everetti.* From Pictou, Nova Scotia:–a, a, a, a, smooth, slender skeleton spicules; b,b,b,b, long smooth, *gemmule* birotulates; c,c, d,d, minute *dermal birotulates*. Collected by A. H. MacKay.

Fig. IV. *Meyenia everetti.* From Gilder Pond, on Mt. Everett, Massachusetts:–a,a,b,b, smooth skeleton spicules; c, c, c *gemmule* birotulates; d, end view of rotule formed of hooked rays; e,e,e, minute *dermal birotulates.* Collected F. Wolle and H. S. Kitchell.

Fig. V. *Meyenia crateriformis.* From Crowe's Mill, Brandywine Creek, Pennsylvania:–a,a, slender, microspined skeleton spicules; b,b,b,b, mature gemmule birotulates with short hooked rays; c,d,e,e, supposed immature forms.

Fig. VI. *Meyenia plumosa,* var. *palmeri.* From the Colorado of the West, Mexico:–a, robust, microspined skeleton spicule; b,c,c spined gemmule birotulates; d,d, rotules of do., irregularly notched; e,e,e, sub-stellate dermal spicules; f. imperfect form of do.; g,g, amorphous, "Scotch terrier" forms.

PLATE XI.

Fig. I. *Heteromeyenia argyrosperma.* From Lehigh Gap, Pennsylvania:–a,a, sparsely microspined skeleton spicules; b, *b,b*, gemmule birotulates of the *longer class*, with one to three hooked rays; *c,c,c,c*, spined birotulates of the *shorter class*.

Fig. II. *Heteromeyenia argyrosperma*, var. *tenuis*. From Harvey's Lake, Pennsylvania:—*a,a,a*, slender skeleton spicules; *b,b,b long* birotulates; *c,c*, birotulates of the *shorter class*; all more slender than in the typical species; *d*, imperfect do.

Fig. III. *Heteromeyenia repens*. From Lehigh Gap, Pennsylvania:—*a,a,a*, microspined skeleton spicules; *b,b*, gemmule birotulates of the *longer* class, with recurved, hooked rays; *c,c,c*, gemmule birotulates of the *shorter* class; *d,d,d*, rotules of do., *e,e*, dermal spicules; *f*. amorphous spicule.

Fig. IV. *Heteromeyenia ryderi*, var. *baleni*. From near Plainfield, New Jersey:—*a,a,a,a*, slender, microspined, skeleton spicules; *b,b,b, long*, hooked, gemmule birotulates; *c,c,c, short* do; with flat rotules; *d,d,d*, surface of last named. Collected by A. D. Balen.

Fig. V. *Heteromeyenia ryderi*, type. From Indian Run, Philadelphia, Pennsylvania:—*a*, skeleton spicule; *b,b,b, long* gemmule birotulates, hooked and spined; *c,c,c,c,c, short* birotulates; *d,d,d*, surface of rotules, margins laciniate, surface microspined or granulated; *e*, amorphous spicule.

Fig. VI. *Heteromeyenia ryderi*, var. *pictovensis*. From Pictou, Nova Scotia:—*a,b,c*, densely spinous skeleton spicules, various terminations; *d,d,d, long* gemmule birotulates; *e,e,e,e, short* do.

PLATE XII.

Fig. I. *Tubella pennsylvanica*. Lehigh Gap, Pennsylvania:—*a,a, a,a*, spined skeleton spicules; *b,b,b*, gemmule "inæquibirotulates," or trumpet-shaped spicules; *c*, group of rotules seen from above, showing the relative sizes of the rotules; *d*, surface of single large rotule.

Fig. II. *Tubella pennsylvanica*, var. *intermedia*. From Indian Run, Philadelphia:—*a,a,a*, stouter skeleton spicules; *b,c,c*, "inæquibirotulates;" *d,e,e*, end view of do. showing comparative size of rotules in this variety.

Fig. III. *Tubella pennsylvanica*, var. *fanshawei*. From Bristol Pond, Pennsylvania:—*a,a,b,b*, skeleton spicules; *c,c,d,d*, birotulates more nearly equal than in either of the former cases, as shown again by–*f,f,g,g*, end views.

Fig. IV. *Carterius tenosperma.* From Lansdowne Run, Philadelphia, Pennsylvania:–*a,a*, skeleton spicules; *b,b,b,c*, spined gemmule birotulates with burr-like rotules; *e,e,e*, ends of do.; *d,d,d,d*, long, spinous, acerate dermal spicules.

Fig. V. *Carterius latitenta.* From Chester Creek, Pennsylvania:– *a,a*, skeleton spicules; *b,b,b,b*, gemmule birotulates, variable in length; *d,d*, face of rotules; *c*, spined *dermals*.

Fig. VI. *Carterius tubisperma.* From Niagara River, near Buffalo, New York:–*a,a*, skeleton spicules; *b,b,b,b,b,d*, gemmule birotulates; *c*, face of rotule; *e,e*, long, spined dermal acerates. Collected by Henry Mills.

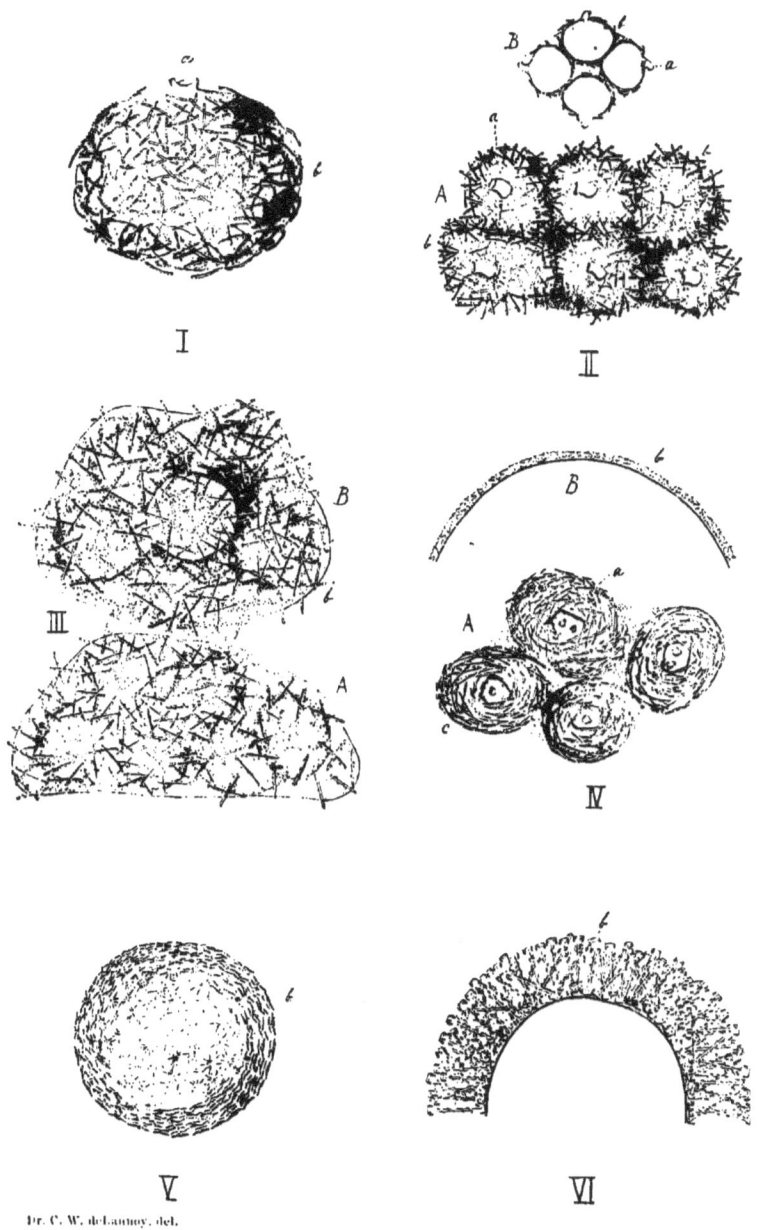

POTTS ON FRESH WATER SPONGES.

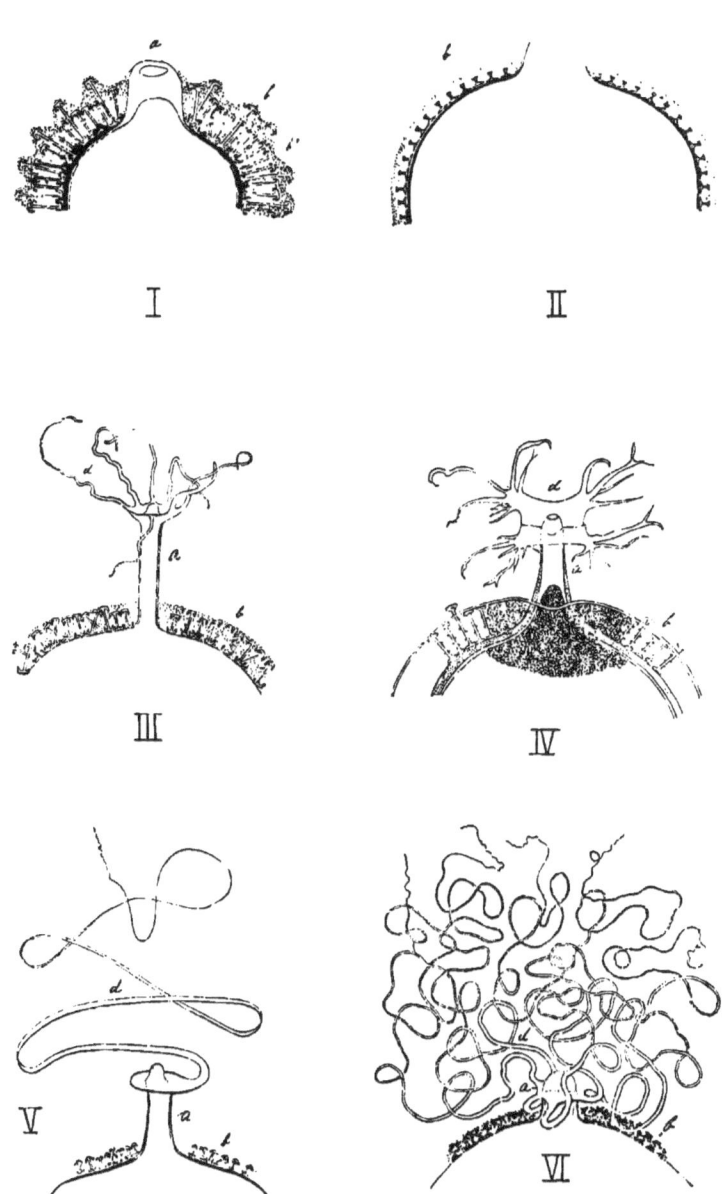

POTTS ON FRESH WATER SPONGES.

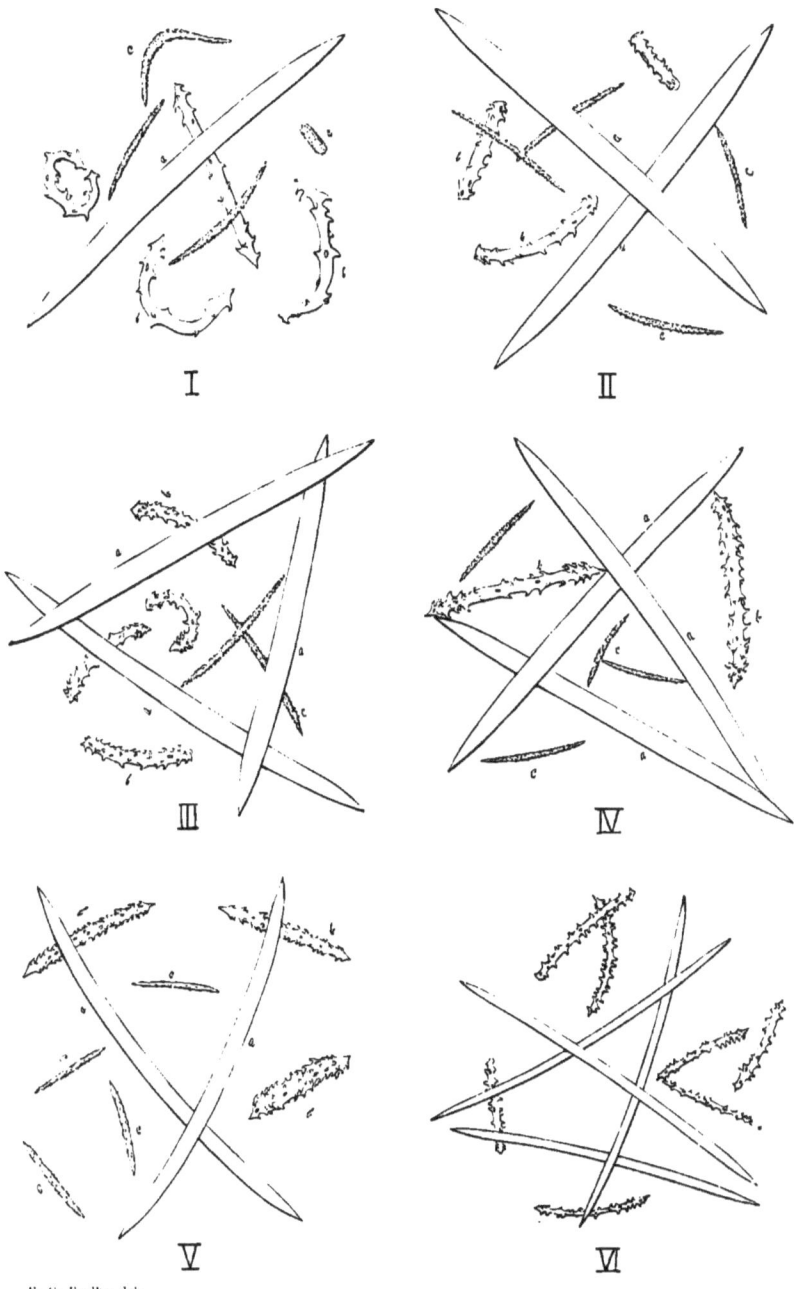

POTTS ON FRESH WATER SPONGES.

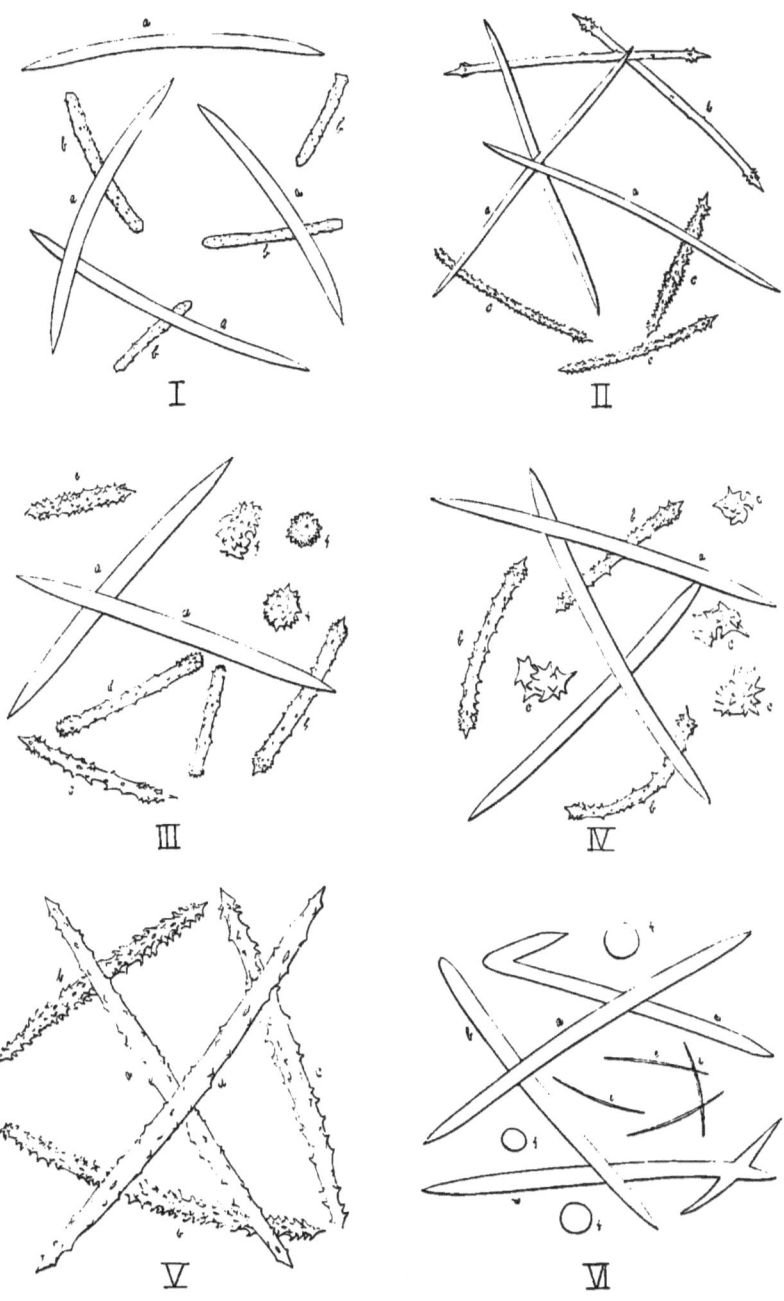

POTTS ON FRESH WATER SPONGES.

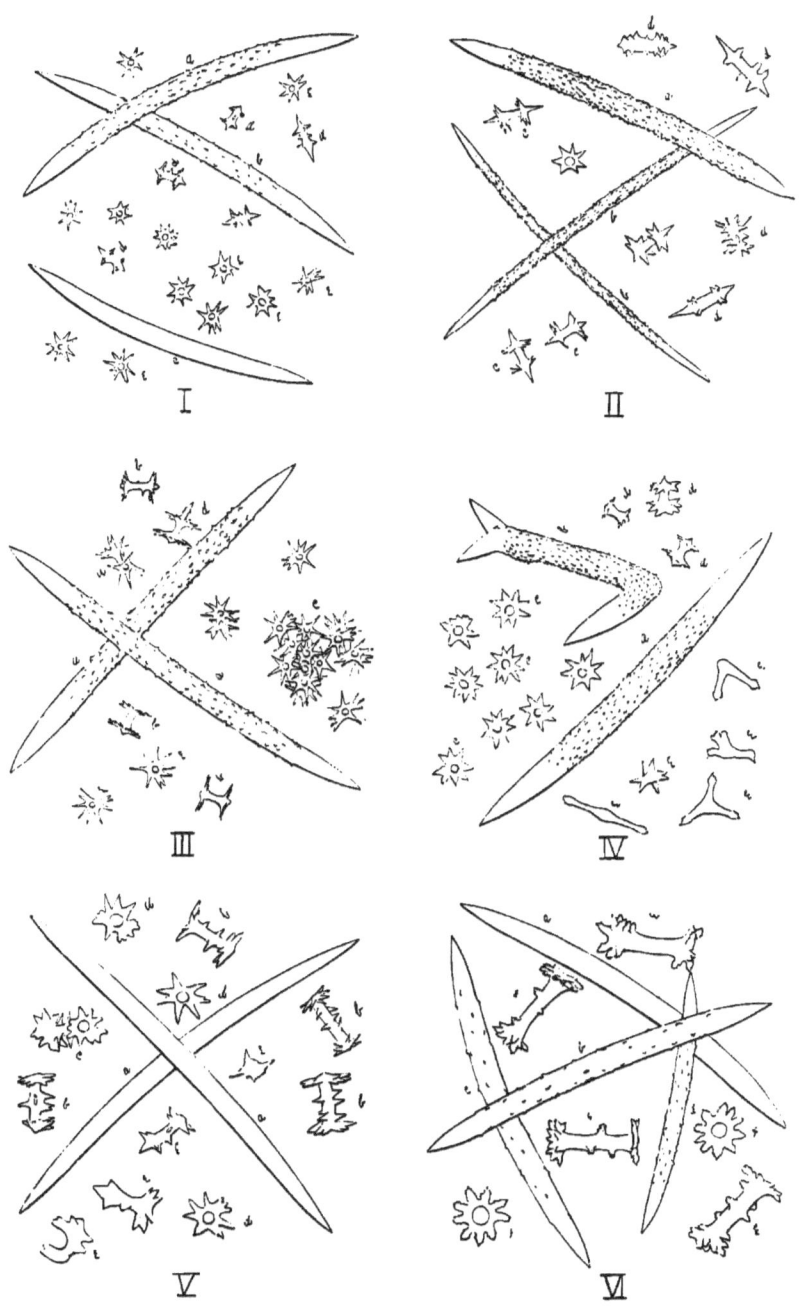

POTTS ON FRESH WATER SPONGES.

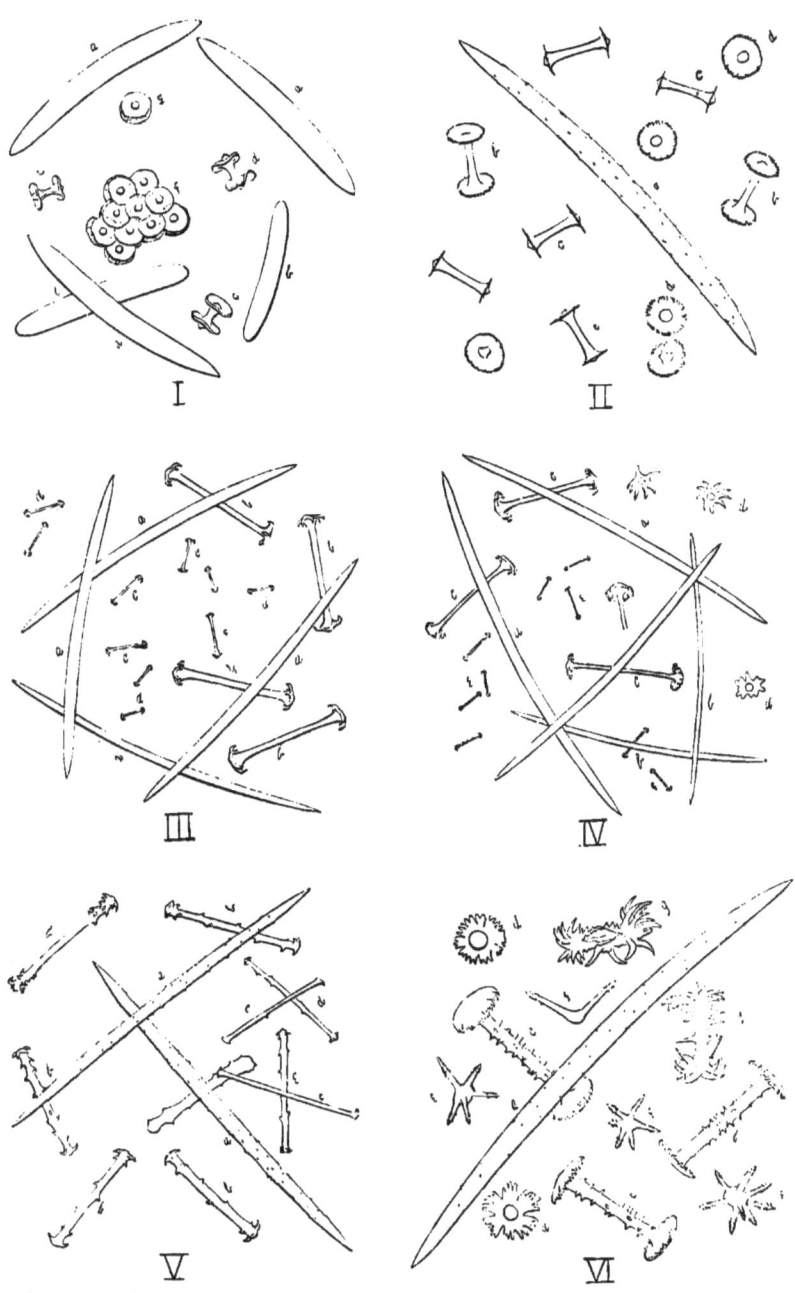

POTTS ON FRESH WATER SPONGES.

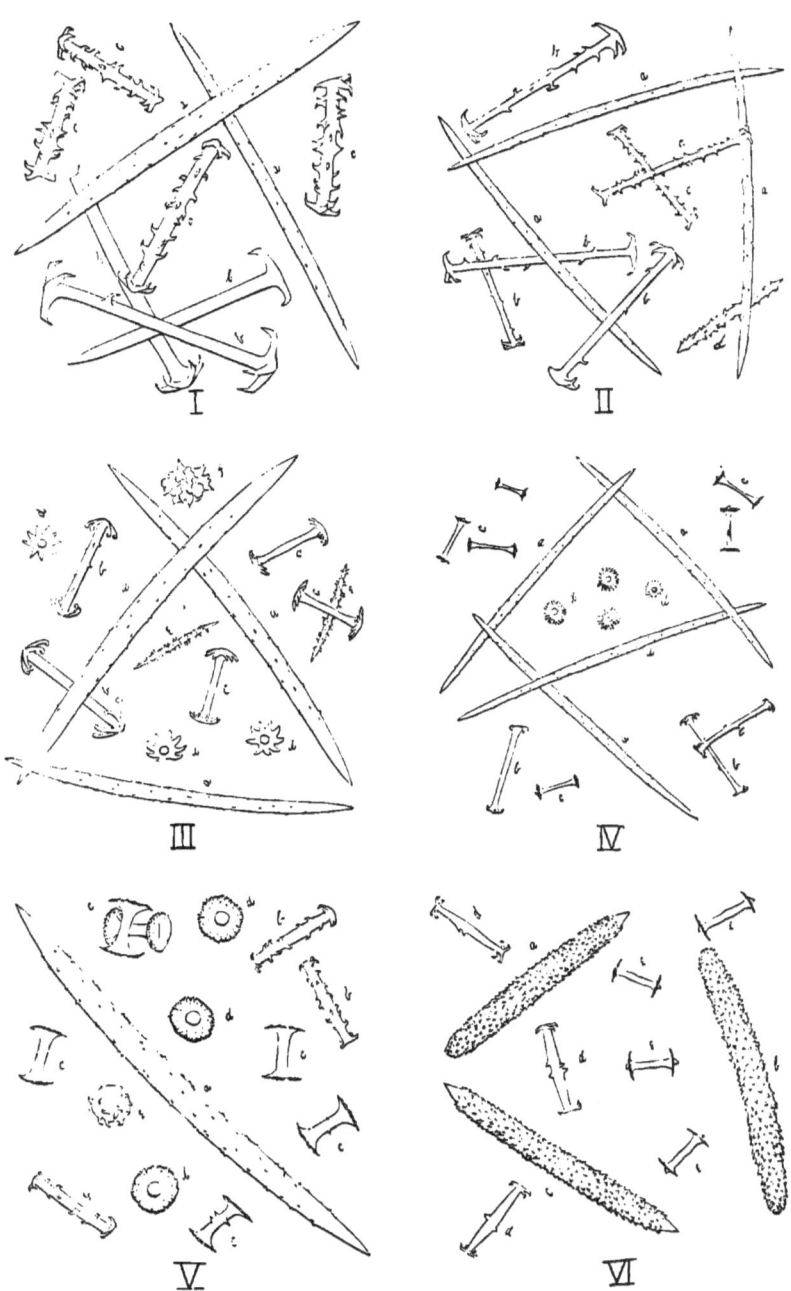

POTTS ON FRESH WATER SPONGES.

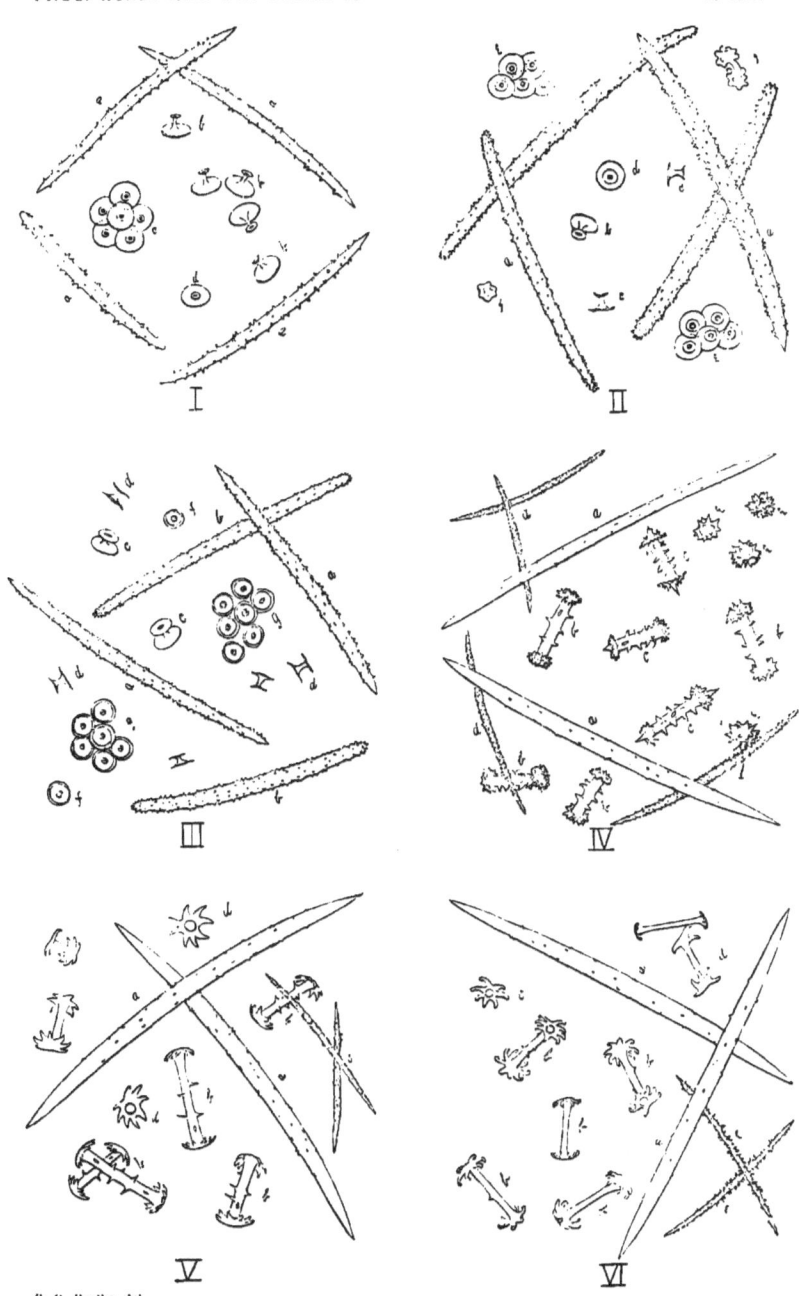

POTTS ON FRESH WATER SPONGES.

www.ingramcontent.com/pod-product-compliance
Lightning Source LLC
Chambersburg PA
CBHW030353170426
43202CB00010B/1359